Supporting Adult Learners through Games and Interactive Teaching
A Practical Guide

Edited by Chandni Hirani and Caroline Varin

LONDON AND NEW YORK

Cover image: © Getty Images

First published 2023
by Routledge
4 Park Square, Milton Park, Abingdon, Oxon OX14 4RN

and by Routledge
605 Third Avenue, New York, NY 10158

Routledge is an imprint of the Taylor & Francis Group, an informa business

© 2023 selection and editorial matter, Chandni Hirani and Caroline Varin; individual chapters, the contributors

The right of Chandni Hirani and Caroline Varin to be identified as the authors of the editorial material, and of the authors for their individual chapters, has been asserted in accordance with sections 77 and 78 of the Copyright, Designs and Patents Act 1988.

All rights reserved. The purchase of this copyright material confers the right on the purchasing institution to photocopy pages which bear the photocopy icon and copyright line at the bottom of the page. No other parts of this book may be reprinted or reproduced or utilised in any form or by any electronic, mechanical, or other means, now known or hereafter invented, including photocopying and recording, or in any information storage or retrieval system, without permission in writing from the publishers.

Trademark notice: Product or corporate names may be trademarks or registered trademarks, and are used only for identification and explanation without intent to infringe.

British Library Cataloguing-in-Publication Data
A catalogue record for this book is available from the British Library

Library of Congress Cataloging-in-Publication Data
Names: Hirani, Chandni, editor. | Varin, Caroline, editor.
Title: Supporting adult learners through games and interactive teaching : a practical guide / Edited by Chandni Hirani and Caroline Varin.
Description: Abingdon, Oxon ; New York, NY : Routledge, 2023. | Includes bibliographical references and index.
Identifiers: LCCN 2022025849 (print) | LCCN 2022025850 (ebook) | ISBN 9781032127941 (hardback) | ISBN 9781032136158 (paperback) | ISBN 9781003230120 (ebook)
Subjects: LCSH: Adult learning. | Educational games--Social aspects. | Interactive multimedia--Study and teaching. | Teaching--Aids and devices. | Motivation in education.
Classification: LCC LC5225.L42 S85 2023 (print) | LCC LC5225.L42 (ebook) | DDC 374/.267--dc23/eng/20220916
LC record available at https://lccn.loc.gov/2022025849
LC ebook record available at https://lccn.loc.gov/2022025850

ISBN: 978-1-032-12794-1 (hbk)
ISBN: 978-1-032-13615-8 (pbk)
ISBN: 978-1-003-23012-0 (ebk)

DOI: 10.4324/9781003230120

Typeset in Times New Roman
by SPi Technologies India Pvt Ltd (Straive)

For Alexia, Adi and Vera – never stop playing

And for the educators striving to make learning fun again

Contents

Acknowledgements ix
Foreword x
About the Authors xiii
List of Contributors xiv

1 **Introduction** 1
CAROLINE VARIN AND CHANDNI HIRANI

2 **Playing 'Against and With': Learning IR Theories by Gaming the Prisoner's Dilemma** 13
NORMA ROSSI

3 **Using Role Play to Teach Learners How to Negotiate Using Different Strategies** 25
CHANDNI HIRANI

4 **Toffeconomy: Creating a Fictional Society to Illustrate Economic Concepts** 32
RUDI ACKERMAN

5 **Pandemics, Popular Culture and Problem-Based Gaming: Teaching State Responses to Disease Control the 'Undead Way'** 38
MALTE RIEMANN

6 **Playful Mocktails Competition©: Developing Empathy** 47
ED GONSALVES

7 **Developing a Strategy to Play Monopoly™ Using Mathematical Techniques and Explore Various Analytical Methods** 58
SAHIL SHAH

8 Reclamation: Game-Based Critical Re-thinking
of Historical First and Bests 81
CHIEDZA MUTSAKA SKYUM AND PUJA SINGH

9 Using Role-Play to Understand the Impacts of Social
Media through Action Research 96
SEQUOYAH WHARTON

10 Games on a Grid (I): Noughts and Crosses 106
PHILIPPA MULLINS

11 Games on a Grid (II): Hotspot 116
RACHEL WARNICK

12 A Fantasy Game to Illustrate the Psychology of Power
and Information Asymmetry 126
RUDI ACKERMAN

13 Building up Trust and Rapport with Neuroscience Insights 135
CAROLA HIEKER

14 Design Thinking for Communication, Planning and
Problem-Solving 141
KASIA HANULA

15 Using an Experiential Activity to Teach Customer Discovery
in Entrepreneurship 154
DEMILADE OLUWASINA

16 Teaching Students How to Network: Goal-Setting,
Maintenance and Technology 163
SVEN BOTHA

17 Conclusion 172

Index 175

Acknowledgements

This book has been made possible thanks to all our contributors who took the time to share their knowledge and experience through their chapters. Their belief in a "Play to Learn" future has allowed us to put together this rich book full of a variety of interesting chapters from all corners of the world.

Thank you to the team and educators at Professors Without Borders. The platform has enabled us to meet so many inspiring education practitioners who have contributed to this volume!

We are particularly grateful to:

Graham for the support with chapter reviews

Ranju, Kapu, Krupa, Umang, Hemal and Aseda for the constant support to make this dream a reality

Vera for whom the future of education is all about play

Our families, for their encouragement, support and patience!

Foreword

Dame Tessy Antony-De Nassau
President and Co-founder Professors Without Borders

As the mother of two school-aged sons and an infant, I have long been preoccupied with how to best educate children. This interest has extended to my work as co-founder and president of the non-governmental organisation Professors Without Borders. What do students need to learn, and which approach is best to facilitate this learning?

The *what* question is often set centrally by governments, who make education compulsory and subsidise it. Naturally, the curriculum follows government interests, whether this is citizenship building, addressing market demands or preparing the next generation of industry and political leaders. Even in private schools, the curriculum seeks to create 'ideal' citizens capable of succeeding personally and professionally with the guidance of a set of tools and values decided by the programme's leadership.

This book does not address the *what* of education. It focuses on the *how*. For what use is there in teaching students material that they do not understand, won't remember or cannot use? While many education policymakers have focused on content, the faculty members are responsible for delivery, although this is often shaped and limited by existing teacher training programmes and resources. I know first-hand how important it is to grab a student's attention and keep it for the duration of the class; why addressing the individual learning styles and difficulties of each student is essential to enable effective learning. My children have wrestled with dyslexia most of their academic lives, and while this does not have to hold them back, it requires compassionate and inclusive teaching. Too many students are left behind by a one-size-fits-all approach to teaching.

As I watch my children play growing up, I appreciate the many benefits: socialising, problem-solving, creativity and imagination, relaxing. And I envy them this time and capacity they have to enjoy themselves so thoroughly while doing something they don't even realise is entirely beneficial. Adults have forgotten to value and reward play. We don't encourage others to play and rarely do we take the time to do so ourselves, despite the proven advantages, as outlined in every chapter you will read here. If schools and parents do not value play, how will employers convince their staff that this is a good way to upskills, as evidenced in all the expensive programmes developed in top private companies that try to stimulate and train employees through interactive games?

Chandni Hirani and Dr Caroline Varin have put together an original and much-needed contribution to the literature on effective teaching. By focusing on 'games' and 'playing' as important pedagogical tools, they draw from the vast body of research lauding experiential learning (Kolb 1984) and interactive learning environments that are growing in vocational training. They extend the science beyond the context of teaching young children or professionals and argue in favour of integrating play into the classrooms, where it has largely been forgotten: from the age of 7 to the day they leave universities, students are taught using largely unitary systems – namely, lecturing with some experiments.

This edited volume benefits from a wide array of experiences, with contributions from educators whose voices have not been heard before on this platform. Successful, experienced, passionate educators from around the world, who have experimented with teaching styles and adapted their methods to include different types of learners, thereby making adult education more fun and relatable. I am personally proud to see so many contributors from the network of Professors Without Borders, an organisation that has, from the start, promoted student-focused and skills-focused education and encouraged a classroom experience that is both equitable and enjoyable. This can only be achieved when educators focus on the *how*, not just on the *what*.

The games shared in this volume also emphasise the importance of skills development, which cannot be gained merely through lectures. Each chapter of this book highlights the skills that students will be practicing, many of which, such as problem-solving and teamwork, are high on the priority list for companies and consultancies employing the workforce needed to build a prosperous future.

Encouraging teachers, especially traditional lecturers, to adapt their style of instruction is audacious and much needed. To be clear, the authors are not arguing for a transformation in teaching, but merely make a sensible and well-rationalised argument in favour of integrating play into classrooms to enable more inclusive and deeper learning.

This book argues for a reset in teaching methodology and ideology, that learning should be enjoyable and interactive throughout life, from childhood to old age, and especially in adult education. This can be achieved by integrating play back into the classrooms that it left as children turned into students.

Finally, this book is uniquely packaged as a manageable manual that is highly structured and user-friendly. Any educator can pick it up, read a few games or learn about the underlying philosophy of learning through play. The games are easy and adaptable to any classroom and many contexts. *Supporting Adult Learners through Games and Interactive Teaching* takes away any excuse for avoiding change and overcomes some of the limitations to introducing games in adult education – namely, a lack of training, time and resources available to modern-day educators.

Tessy is a social entrepreneur, businesswoman, philanthropist, UNAIDSS ambassador, public speaker, activist and mother. She is an associate at LSEideas at the London School of Economics. She is the co-founder of Professors Without Borders, an international education non-profit. Tessy is an ambassador for UNAIDS (Global Advocate for Young Women and Adolescent Girls), as well as a patron to United Nations Association (UNA-UK). Previously, she spent time in the Luxembourg military, during which she was deployed in Kosovo as a peacekeeper and the only woman in her draft. She received the Woman of the Decade award from the Women Economic Forum in January 2017, the Humanities medal for spreading humanistic ideas worldwide and the Global Empowerment Award for her work in Africa.

Kolb, D. (1984) Experiential learning: experience as the source of learning and development. Englewood Cliffs, New Jersey: Prentice Hall.

About the Authors

Chandni Hirani is the Head of Africa Programmes at LSE Generate, the home of entrepreneurship at the London School of Economics. She is also the Accelerator Manager at Katapult VC investing in African Tech start-ups. Her interests lie in developing innovative ways to deliver education outcomes, and she has worked in the education sector across the UK, Kenya, Uganda, Rwanda and Nigeria both through teaching and programme development. She is active in the circular economy sector as well as the start-up ecosystem in Africa and serves on the board of a US-based EdTech operating across USA, Canada and Nigeria.

Caroline Varin is co-founder and CEO of educational charity Professors Without Borders (Prowibo) and Senior Lecturer in international relations at Regent's University London. Caroline is committed to making higher education more equitable, accessible and enjoyable by promoting knowledge-sharing, networking and upskilling. She has published books and articles on international security and spearheaded publications, workshops and conferences on education through Think Tank Without Borders.

Contributors

Rudi Ackerman works as a part-time Lecturer and Research Supervisor at the African Leadership University in Rwanda. Previously, he taught micro- and macroeconomics as a full-time faculty member and designed an interdisciplinary undergraduate political economy course that uses role-playing dynamics to simulate a real-world political landscape. In addition to teaching and researching in the field of development, agriculture and the circular economy, he is also a practitioner working for the INGO One Acre Fund focused on agriculture.

Sven Botha is an Assistant Lecturer in the Department of Politics and International Relations at the University of Johannesburg, South Africa. He teaches undergraduate courses in international law and civil-military relations in Africa and a postgraduate course in gender and politics. Sven has worked and published on gender, responses to terrorism, diplomacy, foreign policy, pedagogy and early career development in the humanities and social sciences. As part of his commitment to early career development, Sven served as the chairperson of the Research Committee on Early-Career Research (2019–2021) for the South African Association of Political Studies and is currently the coordinator of the Masters Forum of the RISC-RISE Consortium.

Ed Gonsalves is Director of the Cooplexity Institute (Barcelona) and specialises in the design, development and delivery of games-based and other learning programmes for high-performance executive teams. He is a European Union (EU) 3E Fellow and UKEE Entrepreneurship Fellow (Practitioner). Ed is Visiting and Associate Professor at Toulouse Business School and ESADE Business School in Barcelona, respectively. His work, research and publications over the last 20 years have focused on corporate and entrepreneurial executive play in decision-making for uncertain and ambiguous settings.

Kasia Hanula is experienced in public policy strategies with more than ten years' experience running successful social impact campaigns and advocating for a wide range of legislative, regulatory and legal challenges. She has an outstanding record of achievement guiding the design, development and implementation of policies and programmes at the European and international levels on issues such as inequalities, financial reforms and digitalisation. She was the European Commission expert advising on the reviews of the European acquis from the social perspective. She is involved in the discussion on the future of work and digital for development at the EU level. She is currently working on a series of workshops aiming at digital transition and teaching digital skills for a social sector.

Carola Hieker has more than 25 years of experience as a Senior Executive Coach and Change Management Consultant in a wide range of industries, and she is the co-founder of 'hilcoaching', a small consultancy boutique. She is Professor of Leadership at Richmond, the American International University and an Honorary Professor for Transformational Leadership at University College London. Her publications in various journals reach out to scholars and practitioners and focus on leadership, coaching, diversity and mentoring, and she recently published a book titled *The Future of Leadership Development – Disruption and the Impact on Megatrends* with Palgrave.

Philippa Mullins is an Assistant Professor at the College of Humanities & Social Sciences of the American University of Armenia, where she teaches in the master's of human rights and social justice degree programme. Her research interests include disability rights, civil society and social movements, with a particular interest in qualitative research methodologies. In the classroom, she is interested in working collaboratively with students through play and discussion to build connections between students' experiences, 'real-world' prompts and material and the concepts and theories being explored. She aims to support students to develop the tools to take a critical eye to the world around them.

Demilade Oluwasina is Faculty for Entrepreneurship and International Business and Trade at the African Leadership University. He also recently led a Digital Transformation and Digital Entrepreneurship Programme in collaboration with the Alibaba Business School. He is a Design Thinking and Human-Centred Design Trainer and Practitioner and uses these methods to deliver action-oriented experiential learning, especially in entrepreneurship education. Demilade founded and runs planbpreneur. com equipping professionals to explore and kickstart entrepreneurial projects. He is also the author of the Planbpreneur book. Demilade's experience spans several years in learning design, corporate training, advertising, digital strategy and project/product management.

Malte Riemann is a Senior Lecturer in the Department of Defence and International Affairs at the Royal Military Academy Sandhurst and a Visiting Fellow at the University of Reading. His research interests lie at the intersection of historical international relations, international political sociology, critical security studies and public health. His work has been published in various peer-reviewed journals, including *Journal for Global*

Security Studies, *Small Wars & Insurgencies*, *Defence Studies*, *Critical Public Health* and *RUSI Journal*.

Norma Rossi is a Senior Lecturer in Defence and International Affairs at Royal Military Academy Sandhurst and a Visiting Research Fellow at the University of Reading. Her research focuses on the multifaceted relationships between violence, subjectivity and the construction of political authority. Norma has designed and delivered courses in international relations and Conflict Management to civilian and security officials in North Africa, the Middle East, South America, the Balkans and the Caucasus, where she also conducted field research.

Sahil Shah is a Chartered Tax Adviser working in London in a practice that encourages increased scientific research and development to be carried out in the UK. While his day job keeps him busy, in his free time, he enjoys thinking about how mathematical techniques can be applied to practical situations. As a keen enthusiast of how learning itself can be made more engaging, he is keen to use board games like Chess and Monopoly as a tool to teach academic concepts to children and adults alike.

Puja Singh is the Lecturer for International Relations and International Development minors at NHL Stenden University for Applied Sciences. Her approach to education focuses on global citizenship and adopting a one-system viewpoint of the world we live in. Her experience as an educator and a researcher draws from her multiple careers in finance, technology and international development. Her research focuses on topics that are intersectional between social sciences, management and technology.

Chiedza Mutsaka Skyum is the Programme Lead for the Global Challenges Faculty at the African Leadership University, a department of faculty ushering African undergraduate students through problem-solving for some of the continent's biggest challenges. Her learning design emphasises 'decoloniality' in education and finding new approaches by disrupting and deconstructing old approaches and challenging power structures. As an adult learning theory enthusiast, she often publishes opinion articles on the future of adult learning both in higher education and in organisational learning and development.

Rachel Warnick is the Director of Programmes at Professors Without Border and the President and Founder of Nature Océan Indien, a Mauritian non-governmental organisation that empowers young people to be active change-makers. She is also a National Geographic Certified Educator and a Teach SDGs Ambassador. As a specialist educator and learning designer who travels the world to deliver intensive programmes that are exciting and engaging, she has worked with many institutions, private and corporate clients in Europe, Africa, the Middle East and Asia. The experience of living in 14 countries on four continents gives a global perspective to her work.

Sequoyah Wharton is an Adjunct Professor in the College of Arts, Communication and Design department at Long Island University – C.W. Post campus and President of Phi Delta Kappa Chapter 1524, Adjunct Professor in the School of Education and Human Services Department at Molloy College and a full-time New York State certified K–12 Art Educator/Broadcast Journalism Teacher at Brentwood High School. His research specialises in the effects of exposure to visual arts programming on the academic outcomes of K–12 students in science, technology, engineering and mathematics subject areas. Awarded the Distinguished School Improvement Award from the high school where he is employed, Dr Wharton has also been chosen to be a part of Public Broadcast Station's Digital Innovator Programme, where he is recognised as a leader in his community by providing strategies in the educational digital arena and leveraging public media platforms to elevate his students' voices. Dr Wharton is also an integral part of the redevelopment of the New York State Visual Arts Content Specialty Test, a test that the New York State Education Department requires educators to pass before receiving certification. His research interest lies in visual arts, interdisciplinary education and educational leadership.

1 Introduction

Caroline Varin and Chandni Hirani

1.1 Introduction

Game design is a multi-billion-dollar industry, with highly paid specialists who are trained to create the 'perfect' games that educate and motivate students. In real time, however, many classrooms are led by underpaid and overworked teachers who have little training and time for developing and researching games to enhance students' learning. Reduced budgets, higher student enrolment numbers (especially in higher education) and low teacher retention and morale invariably lead to a dearth of games-based learning, regardless of its documented benefits. This book is for those students and teachers. A user-friendly volume of games that can be transferred and adapted to various academic disciplines, require no training or financing and that help develop practical skills while engaging students in rewarding experiences.

Our contributors are all educators from around the world who have generously shared the games they have used in their classrooms. Many are part of the Professors Without Borders network and have taught students in the most complex environments. We share a passion for teaching, engaging students in academics and developing their transferable skills. This edited volume is the result of tried and tested experiences using games-based learning in higher education to motivate and educate our students, no matter where they are, how many there are or what resources they have access to.

1.2 Why Is Play Important? – The Neuro-learning Argument

There is no agreed-upon definition for 'play', especially as this relates to different species, contexts and cultures (Cohen 2006, 18). Roger Caillois describes play as "free (non-obligatory), uncertain (not predetermined), and unproductive (for its own sake)" (2001). This would suggest that the learning that occurs through play is unpredictable and arguably uncontrollable. Indeed, children often identify play in terms of the freedom it affords, specifically from adults (Einarsdóttir 2014). Gray on the other hand argues that play is valued for its means rather than its ends (2017), suggesting that the process of playing is more important than the outcome it incurs,

DOI: 10.4324/9781003230120-1

including the pursuit of learning particular skills. In Western societies, play is largely considered the opposite of work, something to be earned once the 'to-do' list is complete. Consequently, play has been systematically undervalued in work-centric environments including in many educational settings (Sutton-Smith 1970).

The early 20th century saw developments in play research and the neurological benefits of this activity. Indeed, over 3,000 articles investigating the relevance of play have been published in the last 20 years (van Leeuwen and Westwood 2008). Most mammals, especially humans, are born knowing how to play. This skill is natural, instinctive and necessary to develop (learn) the tools needed for survival (Pellegrini et al. 2007). Spinka et al. argue that play enables animals "to develop flexible kinematic and emotional responses to unexpected events in which they experience a sudden loss of control (…and) enhance (their) ability to cope emotionally with unexpected stressful situations" (Spinka et al. 2001). Playing is described as a sequence of events where the player is at times in control and at times out of control, creating a cognitively complex emotional state that we call 'having fun'. Not only does playing have motivational value derived from the enjoyment of the activity, but it also trains the body and the brain of players, enabling them to adapt to new experiences. The physical benefits of play peak in young children around primary school age, but the cognitive benefits can be developed for much longer (Smith and Pellegrini 2008).

The value of play for children is well-documented. The intrinsic ability and motivation for play makes for fertile teaching ground that has subsequently been explored and implanted broadly in Western educational settings targeting young children. This play-to-teach approach however is progressively abandoned in secondary school and disappears nearly completely in adult education. Yet playing continues to be associated with neurological benefits in adults: play releases endorphins, bringing joy and reducing the prevalence of depression and other mental health problems (Ferguson and Kilburn 2010). Playing has also been shown to increase the size of the brain in adult rats: in her 1964 study, Diamond demonstrated that play improves memory and stimulates the growth of the cerebral cortex. In adults, play is integrated into many treatments for Alzheimer's and Dementia due to its documented therapeutic and cognitive benefits (Gottlieb 2003). Significantly for 21st-century skills, play has been shown to stimulate creativity through divergent thinking (Russ 2016; Guilford et al. 1968). This is particularly true for adults who are able to improve on their knowledge base to integrate old ideas into new ways that lead to the creation of new products (Wallas 1926).

There is invariably a strong neuro-learning argument to be made for the importance of play in learning for both children and adults. Play is demonstrably a natural instinct that helps with training the body and the mind throughout life. Conversely, the absence of play can have significant ramifications, as demonstrated by Brown and Vaughan (2010) who observed that missing play in early childhood was one of the single most important variables in predicting criminal and antisocial behaviour. It would be interesting to find out whether this trend can be reversed by reinstating play in adult life to address behavioural problems, or whether the missed opportunity for learning through play is irrevocable.

The next part of this chapter will examine the shortcomings of adult education in a system without play.

1.3 The Limitations of a Vanilla Higher Education

There are many forms and venues for teaching adults, but universities remain the classic benchmark for adult learning in most contemporary societies. In these universities, lecturing prevails as the most cost and time-effective mode of transmitting knowledge from teacher to student. Percival and Ellington (1988) describe the lecture as a "didactic instructional method, involving one-way communication from the active presenter to the more or less passive audience".

Lecturing is not only the prevalent manner of instruction in higher education, but it also has a long history dating back at least to the Ancient Greeks (Matiru et al. 1995). In the absence of the printing press, for universities in the Christian and Muslim medieval times, lecturing served as an important means to pass on knowledge across the ages. The term *lecturing* originates in the Latin word *legere*, meaning to read out loud. While lecturing has dominated the ages, it has by no means precluded discussion or challenges to the lecturer's thoughts. The Socratic method is an established teaching practice that involves a shared dialogue between teacher and student, led by a teacher posing thought-provoking questions, thereby fostering critical thinking and establishing deeper learning.

Reviewing the literature on the effectiveness of lecturing, Matiru et al. (1995) conclude the following:

1) "Lecturing it the most common method used" in adult education.
2) "It is as effective as any other method for imparting knowledge up to comprehension level".
3) "Lectures tend to encourage 'surface' learning only", which depends on memorisation.
4) It is less effective for developing analytical, critical, problem-solving and creative skills.
5) "It is less effective for teaching practical skills than demonstrations and laboratory work".
6) "Discussions are more effective than lectures for changing attitudes".

Furthermore, not everyone learns in the same manner. While students can gain access to the information imparted by the lecturer, they each interpret and understand the content within their own abilities and experiences. This process is further dependent on the quality of the lecture and the ability of the lecturer to answer questions and explain concepts. Lecturers can today count on the historical track record to legitimise this manner of teaching in addition to the availability of new media, technological devices and known lecturing methods that can amplify the message, reinvigorate the experience and stimulate students. The much-lauded Ted Talks are an example of the success and effectiveness of lecturing as a recognised method for sharing knowledge (Friesen 2011).

In many universities, however, lecturers are part of a research community, where their main source of revenue and professional advancement is derived from their publishing record, not their teaching ability. As a result, few lecturers consider themselves *educators* first and foremost. While this doesn't necessarily limit their skills as a lecturer, it does suggest that lecturing or teaching skills are not always one of the criteria for employment or retention of lecturers. In addition to the existing known limitations of the lecture as a method of teaching, the lack of importance given to lecturing skills by institutions of higher education can further diminish the learning experience of students in university education.

1.4 The Demand for 21st-Century Skills

As demonstrated earlier, university lectures are effective for passing on knowledge, relying on memorisation and repetition for students to retain and reproduce said knowledge in their professional environments. This idea dominated much of the pedagogical thinking for higher education in the 20th century. But the role of universities is arguably to prepare students to thrive in their imminent and future careers. Transformations in digital and artificial intelligence (AI) technologies, accelerated by the COVID-19 epidemic, have changed the way we work. This has revealed a serious skills gap. McKinsey, for example, found that as many as "375 million workers globally might have to change occupations in the next decade to meet companies' needs" and "nearly nine in ten executives and managers say their organizations either face skill gaps already or expect gaps to develop within the next five years". Furthermore, a 2020 Udemy report found that on average one in four respondents (25%) believe their education does not prepare them for today's workplace, and in France, fewer than half the surveyed population agreed that they had the skills necessary to keep or find work (Table 1.1).

Companies have coped by using strategies including upskilling, hiring, contracting, redeploying and firing, with skills-building considered to be the most effective way to close the skills gap in the near future. Defining these skills is complex, but in general, all graduates and employees will need to be able to "add value beyond what can be done by automated systems and intelligent machines; operate in a digital environment; and continually adapt to new ways of working". Another McKinsey large-N survey found a direct correlation between higher education attainment and proficiency in cognitive and digital skills; however, in-demand skills such as creativity and imagination, risk-taking, empathy, resolving conflicts, coping with uncertainty and digital ethics were negatively correlated to education. Some skills, it appears, are not taught using prevalent pedagogical methods in university settings.

Table 1.1 21st-Century World Economic Forum

Foundational Literacy	Competences	Character Qualities
How students apply core skills to everyday tasks	*How students approach complex challenges*	*How students approach their changing environment*
Literacy	Critical thinking/problem-solving	Curiosity
Numeracy	Creativity	Initiative
Scientific literacy	Communication	Persistence
Information communications technology literacy	Collaboration	Adaptability
Financial literacy		Leadership
Cultural and civic literacy		Social and cultural awareness

This corroborates our previous findings on the use and shortcomings of lecturing and supports research promoting games and experiential learning as effective and relevant learning tools for adult education.

1.5 The Case for Teaching with Games in Adult Education

While universities have proven themselves to be generally adept at building foundational literacy such as cognitive and digital skills in students, their track record in developing competencies and character qualities, as defined by the World Economic Forum, is less clear. Blackwell et al. (2001) argue that the latter skills are best acquired using experiential learning. By simulating real-world learning experiences, educators can bring the student to engage beyond the theory by providing a context (*experience*) in which the learner has to work collaboratively, synthesise and generate new knowledge to solve problems in a risk-free simulation. A process of self-reflection and timely feedback will also help develop important skills as students critically approach their performance and that of their peers with the view of identifying areas for improvement (Kolb 1984; Hattie 2008).

Experiential learning has grown in popularity in higher education and in business settings. Since Kolb designed his experiential learning model in 1984, the concept has been picked up, developed and lauded by major companies including Deloitte and Manulife, who offer training in AI and analytics for executives specifically using real-life business opportunities and challenges to stimulate optimum learning in a demographic that is often resistant to formal education. The appeal of experiential goes beyond skills-building; it includes the integrative nature of learning-by-doing that empowers students from minority groups with generally fewer opportunities (Cantor 1995, 89), it has motivational power, especially for mature learners, and an important democratic dividend: experiential learning can be created with relatively few resources, making it accessible to underfunded institutions (Cantor 1995, 84).

Despite the growing success of experiential learning in business schools and industry training, it has faced challenges integrating the formal curriculum. Successfully integrating experiential learning into classrooms requires funding for training the teachers, rethinking the design of classes and may need to take time away from didactic learning (lecturing). The advantages of in-depth applied learning need to be balanced against the demands for content and breadth of knowledge. It also requires a shift in attitudes and expectations at all levels, from the policymakers, to the university board, to the educators, students and parents. Despite Cantor's optimistic argument that experiential learning is accessible to all, it remains that shifting learning paradigms requires time, training and funding.

Games-based teaching in this context may therefore be an attractive option that bridges the need for knowledge with the cognitive and motivational advantage of learning-by-doing or in this case learning-by-playing. Without displacing experiential learning, games offer a parenthesis within traditional and non-traditional modes of teaching in a realistic and time-limited framework. Archives of pre-designed games specific by subject and skill can provide educators with existing pre-tested activities that inspire quick adaptation and integration into their course material, with minimum effort and required resources. The use of games for young children has been long-established; their effectiveness in improving student participation and motivation is evidence-based. Furthermore, they have a clear impact on social and emotional learning, two skills that are increasingly in demand and statistically declining in young digitally educated employees. The case for continuing learning with games beyond the playground to secondary schools and in university instruction is undeniable.

1.6 Future Directions

The biggest obstacle to change in education is funding. The second biggest is time. The first is difficult to change, as it requires budgetary considerations, often at the national level. Those who need it the most, whether in countries with fewer resources, rural areas that are often overlooked or institutions that cling to their traditions will find the obstacle insurmountable. Time is arguably equally challenging – a shift in pedagogical approach requires that educators find time to reflect, research and experiment. In a world with increasing pressures on teachers, whether research or administrative requirements, time is the least available commodity.

So, what can be done?

The first step in effecting change in teaching practices is to target the people becoming teachers. Training at this stage is a requirement and there is time to learn. Future teachers should be the first port of call for instructing pedagogical knowledge and methods such as experiential learning and games-based learning. This is the most cost-efficient approach to change, although it can be relatively slow to integrate cross-generationally. It also does not address the impending challenge of the skills gap.

Upskilling opportunities for educators and lecturers could be built into the promotion ladder, although once more, this requires time and would come at the expense of something else. In order for this approach to be effective, there needs to be incentive and real benefits to participants in addition to political will. Training opportunities, especially for experienced educators, are wasted if they are not carried out to a high standard.

Another option is to fund and distribute easy-to-use teaching manuals adapted by subject to alleviate the teaching burden. These should be hard copy and freely available to educators. However, this option is negatively affected by the high cost of purchase and distribution rights held by many academic publishers. Open-access resources, particularly those that promote effective teaching and address known market needs, should be promoted and ring-fenced by the Department of Education.

This book goes one step in that direction. We value the limited time that educators have, their vast experience in teaching and their curiosity to learn from each other.

1.7 How to Use This Book

This book is a valuable toolkit for educators looking for a practical manual that can be used without needing any prior knowledge of games-based learning pedagogy. It consists of 13 unique and individual games that teach various skills across a range of difficulty levels. Each chapter starts with a brief pedagogical explanation detailing why interactive and games-based learning is suitable for the skills that are outlined in that chapter. This provides the educator with a deeper understanding of the logic of the chapter as well as a better appreciation for the interactive method described and outlined in the game. Conversely, educators who are primarily interested in the application of the game and not in the pedagogy behind it can directly engage with the game section of each chapter without needing to read the pedagogical explanations. Each chapter has a set of detailed instructions explaining how the educator should set up the game, as well as how to instruct and guide students throughout the game. All relevant material and handouts needed by the learners are provided in the chapter, which educators can print or photocopy.

While all the chapters consist of individual games, some of the chapters are complementary in nature and games across multiple chapters can be played in sequence to deepen the students' learning of a particular skill. The high-level skills covered in the book include strategy, decision-making, problem-solving, critical thinking, teamwork, leadership, creative thinking and communication. These skills are taught through various contexts within the fields of economics, business, international relations and governance, as well as a few games that are field agnostic. The skills are taught within a specific context in one discipline, for example, the skill of problem-solving taught through a pandemic crisis management game within the field of international relations. Given this context-specific nature of the games, learners are able to immediately understand the application of the skill, as they are not engaging with it through a theoretical lens but by immersing themselves practically and immediately into the skill. Playing the complimentary games in sequence will further enable learners to apply the skills they attain across different contexts and fields, allowing them to gain the ability to transfer their skills onwards. The next section will outline the skills taught in the various chapters, as well as which chapters consist of complimentary games.

1.8 Synopsis

Chapters 2, 3 and 7 have a strong focus on developing the skills of strategy and decision-making through the three different fields of international relations, business and finance. Chapters 2 and 3 have a medium complexity, while Chapter 7 has a high complexity. The games used in these chapters are a prisoner's dilemma role play, an employment negotiation and a game of Monopoly. Each game can be played individually based on the context the educator is focusing on. The games are also complementary and can be played in the sequence of Chapter 2, 3 and then 7. Chapter 2 lays the foundation for understanding the basic tenets of decision-making, Chapter 3 applies this skill to a real-world scenario of an employment negotiation and Chapter 7 provides a more complex environment with multiple variables through the game of Monopoly. Playing these three games in sequence will deepen the learner's decision-making skills, as well as teach a range of additional skills such as data analysis, critical thinking, international relations theories and negotiation strategies.

Chapters 2, 5, 8 and 12 have a strong focus on developing skills within the field of social sciences. All four chapters have a medium complexity. The contexts of these four chapters include prisoner cooperation, pandemic crisis management, social history and asymmetrical group power dynamics. Each game can be played individually based on the specific context that the educator is focusing on. The games are also complementary and can be played in any sequence, with all the games having medium complexity. Playing these games one after the other will introduce skills in problem-solving, crisis management, critical inquiry and group dynamics through four different contexts of international relations. Given the four different contexts within international relations, playing these four games in sequence provides an educator focusing only on international relations, for example, the opportunity to ensure learners gain skills from a multi-dimensional perspective from within the same field. Each chapter can also be played individually without needing to sequentially play all chapters.

Chapters 4 and 7 have a strong focus on developing skills within the fields of finance and economics. Chapter 4 has a medium complexity, while Chapter 7 has a high complexity. Each game can be played individually based on the context the educator is focusing on. Both chapters look at developing decision-making skills through understanding money, inflation and supply and demand. They are excellent complimentary chapters and should be played in the sequence of Chapter 4 followed by Chapter 7. Each chapter can also be played individually without needing to sequentially play both chapters.

Chapters 6, 10, 11, 13 and 16 have a strong focus on developing students' trust-building, empathy and communication skills. All games are of low complexity and provide a range of interactive approaches to quickly and easily learn these skills. Each of these games can be used as an introductory session to capture the attention of a class at the start of a course or module, making them very suitable as ice-breaker games due to their low complexity. Chapters 10, 11 and 13 in particular lend very well to introductory sessions as they are not focused on any particular field; therefore, this provides educators with the flexibility to use these games across most modules and fields. Chapter 6 makes a valuable complimentary session to Chapters 10, 11 and 13 as it focuses on the context of a start-up and would support the deepening of the skills through its context-specific nature. Chapter 16 focuses on developing the skill of networking, which is considered a life skill and can be played as a complimentary game to any of the games in this book. Each chapter can also be played individually without needing to sequentially play all chapters.

Chapters 6 and 15 both focus on building customer empathy, creativity and product development under the entrepreneurship theme. They are both of low complexity and are complementary given that they both focus on entrepreneurs understanding their customers and lead to some level of product ideation/development. The chapters can be played individually without needing to play both chapters, or they can both be played in order to deepen the skills through the exposure of the different contexts.

Chapters 9 and 14 have a strong focus on action research and design thinking. Both games have medium complexity. These chapters are complementary as both of them are centred around active listening and understanding a problem through the concept of design thinking. For a complimentary approach, Chapter 14 should be taught followed by Chapter 9. Chapter 14 provides a foundational understanding through a series of short interactive games, while Chapter 9 provides the context of social media action research to deepen these skills. Each chapter can also be played individually without needing to sequentially play both chapters.

The complementary approach described thus far is one example of how the chapters add value to each other either through overlapping skills or common disciplines. Given the wide range of skills that are taught across the chapters, educators using this book should freely find alternative combinations of complementary chapters based on their teaching styles and content they are teaching. Educators should also freely modify the games to suit different contexts. For example, educators teaching action research can take the game outlined in Chapter 9 and change the context of social media to their relevant context while leaving the rest of the game's instruction intact. Additionally, Chapter 3 outlines different contexts at the end of the chapter that the game can apply to. This context adaptation can be done with all the games outlined in the book.

The intention is to allow educators to use the games in the book as a base structure. They do not need to spend time developing games from scratch but instead can focus on delivering the game to learners in the format already outlined in the book or by making small contextual adaptations. Educators are also able to integrate, increase or decrease the use of technology to play the games based on the access and resources available to their students. For example, educators using Chapter 6 can introduce online whiteboarding tools such as Miro if students are online and have access to it. Alternatively, they can use physical tools such as flip charts as outlined in the chapter. As educators become familiar with the games, they can begin to increase or decrease the complexity of the games by introducing new variables they feel are relevant to the skills and context already outlined in the chapters.

This book should be considered an easy-to-use manual that helps educators integrate games into their classes, thereby improving motivation levels, diversifying and solidifying skill sets, and generally making use of all the psychological and neurological benefits that games can bring to adult users.

Bibliography

Agrawal, S., de Smet, A. and Poplawski, P. (2020). *How companies are reskilling to address skill gaps|McKinsey*. [online] www.mckinsey.com. Available at: https://www.mckinsey.com/business-functions/people-and-organizational-performance/our-insights/beyond-hiring-how-companies-are-reskilling-to-address-talent-gaps

Blackwell, A., Bowes, L., Harvey, L., Hesketh, A.J. and Knight, P.T. (2001). Transforming work experience in higher education. *British Educational Research Journal*, [online] 27(3), pp. 269–85. Available at: https://onlinelibrary.wiley.com/doi/abs/10.1080/01411920120048304

Brown, S.L. and Vaughan, C.C. (2010). *Play: how it shapes the brain, opens the imagination, and invigorates the soul*. New York: Avery.

Caillois, R. (2001). *Man, play and games*. Urbana, IL: University Of Illinois Press; Wantage.

Cantor, J. (1995). *Experiential learning in higher education: linking classroom and community*. Eric Publications. https://eric.ed.gov/?id=ED404949

Cohen, D. (2006). *The development of play*. London: Routledge.

Cowan, K. (2020). *A panorama of play digital futures commission*. [online] London: 5Rights Foundation. Available at: https://digitalfuturescommission.org.uk/wp-content/uploads/2020/10/A-Panorama-of-Play-A-Literature-Review.pdf

Deloitte (2020). *The upskilling imperative building a future-ready workforce for the AI age*. https://www2.deloitte.com/content/dam/Deloitte/ca/Documents/deloitte-analytics/ca-covid19-upskilling-EN-AODA.pdf

Dewar, G. (2014). The cognitive benefits of play: effects on the learning brain. [online] *Parenting Science*. Available at: https://parentingscience.com/benefits-of-play/

Dondi, M., Klier, J., Panier, F. and Schubert, J. (2021). *Future-citizen skills | McKinsey*. [online] www.mckinsey.com. Available at: https://www.mckinsey.com/Industries/Public-and-Social-Sector/Our-Insights/Defining-the-skills-citizens-will-need-in-the-future-world-of-work

Einarsdóttir, J. (2014). Children's perspectives on play. In: *SAGE handbook of play and learning in early childhood*. Thousand Oaks, CA: SAGE Publications, Chapter 26. https://sk.sagepub.com/reference/the-sage-handbook-of-play-and-learning-in-early-childhood/n27.xml

Ferguson, C.J. and Kilburn, J. (2010). Much ado about nothing: the misestimation and overinterpretation of violent video game effects in Eastern and Western nations: comment on Anderson et al. (2010). *Psychological Bulletin*, 136(2), pp. 174–78.

Forti, A., Meierkord, A. and Vandeweyer, M. (2019). *Getting skills right: future-ready adult learning systems | en | OECD | OCDE*. [online] www.oecd.org. Available at: https://www.oecd.org/fr/publications/getting-skills-right-future-ready-adult-learning-systems-9789264311756-en.htm [Accessed 3 January 2022].

Friesen, N. (2011). The lecture as a transmedial pedagogical form. *Educational Researcher*, 40(3), pp. 95–102.

Gottlieb, S. (2003). Mental activity may help prevent dementia. *BMJ*, 326(7404), p. 1418. ncbi.nlm.nih.gov/pmc/articles/PMC1151037/#:~:text=Participating%20in%20mentally%20challenging%20leisure,dementia%20than%20other%20elderly%20people

Gray, P. (2017). What exactly is play, and why is it such a powerful vehicle for learning? *Topics in language disorders*, [online] 37(3), pp. 217–28. Available at: https://www.psychologytoday.com/sites/default/files/what_is_play_published.pdf

Guilford, J.P., Hendricks, M. and Hoepfner, R. (1968). Solving social problems creatively*. *The Journal of Creative Behavior*, 2(3), pp. 155–64.

Hattie, J. (2008). *Visible learning: a synthesis of over 800 meta-analyses relating to achievement*. Abingdon, Oxon: Taylor & Francis Ltd.

Hopper, T. (2002). Teaching games for understanding: the importance of student emphasis over content emphasis. *Journal of Physical Education, Recreation & Dance*, 73(7), pp. 44–8.

Juan, A.A., Loch, B., Daradoumis, T. and Ventura, S. (2017). Games and simulation in higher education. *International Journal of Educational Technology in Higher Education* [online], 14(1). Available at: https://educationaltechnologyjournal.springeropen.com/articles/10.1186/s41239-017-0075-9 [Accessed 21 January 2020].

Koeners, M.P. and Francis, J. (2020). The physiology of play: potential relevance for higher education. *International Journal of Play*, 9(1), pp. 143–59.

Kolb, D.A. (1984). *Experimental learning: experience as the source of learning and development* [online]. London: Prentice-Hall. Available at: https://www.researchgate.net/publication/235701029_Experiential_Learning_Experience_As_The_Source_Of_Learning_And_Development

Liberal Education (2009). *The power of experiential education* [online]. Association of American Colleges & Universities. Available at: https://www.aacu.org/publications-research/periodicals/power-experiential-education

Liu, C., Solis, S., Jensen, H., Hopkins, E., Neale, D., Zosh, J., Hirsh-Pasek, K. and Whitebread, D. (2017). *November 2017 neuroscience and learning through play: a review of the evidence white paper* [online]. Available at: https://www.legofoundation.com/media/1064/neuroscience-review_web.pdf

Matiru, B., Mwangi, A., Schlette, R., Deutsche Stiftung Für Internationale Entwicklung. Zentralstelle Für Erziehung, Wissenschaft Und Dokumentation and University of Kassel. Institute for Socio-Cultural Studies. (1995). *Teach your best: a handbook for university lecturers*. Bonn: German Foundation For International Development, Education, Science And Documentation Centre.

Pellegrini, A.D., Dupuis, D. and Smith, P.K. (2007). Play in evolution and development. *Developmental Review*, 27(2), pp. 261–76.

Pellegrini, A.D. and Smith, P.K. (1998). Physical activity play: the nature and function of a neglected aspect of play. *Child Development*, 69(3), pp. 577–98.

Percival, F. and Ellington, H. (1988). *A handbook of educational technology*. London: K. Page Nichols.

Russ, S.W. (2003). Play and creativity: developmental issues. *Scandinavian Journal of Educational Research*, 47(3), pp. 291–303.

Russ, S.W. (2016). Pretend play: antecedent of adult creativity. *New Directions for Child and Adolescent Development*, 2016(151), pp. 21–32.

Schwartz, M. (2021). *Best practices in experiential learning* [online]. Available at: https://www.mcgill.ca/eln/files/eln/doc_ryerson_bestpracticesryerson.pdf

Secretary of State for Education and Skills (2003). *2003 white paper higher ed* [online]. Secretary of State for Education and Skills. Available at: http://www.educationengland.org.uk/documents/pdfs/2003-white-paper-higher-ed.pdf

Siviy, Stephen M. (2016). A brain motivated to play: insights into the neurobiology of playfulness. *Behaviour*, 153(6–7), pp. 819–44.

Smith, P. and Pellegrini, A. (2008). Learning through play. In: Gallagher, R. J., Mora-Flores, E. R., and Selmi, A. M. *Early childhood curriculum for all learners: integrating play and literacy activities*. Thousand Oaks, CA: SAGE Publication, pp. 29–55.

Somers, J.A. and Holt, M.E. (1993). What's in a game? A study of games as an instructional method in an adult education class. *Innovative Higher Education*, 17(4), pp. 243–57.

Spinka, M., Newberry, R.C. and Bekoff, M. (2001). Mammalian play: training for the unexpected. *The Quarterly Review of Biology*, 76(2), pp. 141–68.

Sutton-Smith, B. (1970). Psychology of childlore: the triviality barrier. *Western Folklore*, 29(1), p. 1.

Udemy (2020). *2019/2020 Skills gap report*. https://research.udemy.com/wp-content/uploads/2020/09/Skills-Gap-Report-2019_2020-2021-Rebrand-v2-gs.pdf

van Leeuwen, L. and Westwood, D. (2008). Adult play, psychology and design. *Digital Creativity*, 19(3), pp. 153–61.

Wallas, G. (1926). *Art of thought*. London: J. Cape.

Whitton, N. (2013). Games for learning. *International Review of Qualitative Research*, 6(3), pp. 424–39.

Whitton, N. and Langan, M. (2018). Fun and games in higher: an analysis of UK student perspectives. *Teaching in Higher Education*, 24(8), pp. 1–14.

Wright, S., McNeill, M., Fry, J. and Wang, J. (2005). Teaching teachers to play and teach games. *Physical Education & Sport Pedagogy*, 10(1), pp. 61–82.

2 Playing 'Against and With'
Learning IR Theories by Gaming the Prisoner's Dilemma

Norma Rossi

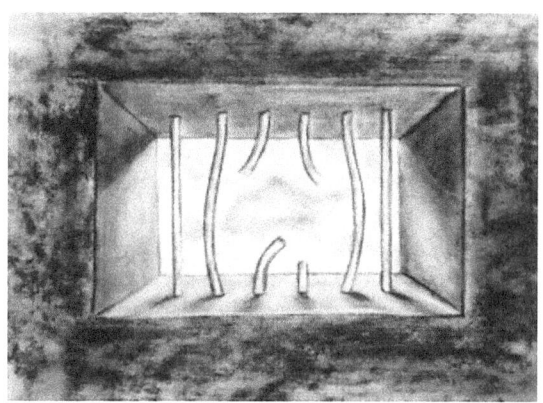

2.1 Overview

Teaching international relations (IR) theories in an engaging way that fuels students' curiosity and understanding is often challenging. In-class games are an excellent way of achieving this, which is shown via a game based on an adapted version of the prisoner's dilemma. The game described in this chapter provides an intuitive entry into the roles of rationality and emotions in IR, as well as the explanatory and constitutive character of IR theories.

The use of games-based learning has acquired increasing importance in tertiary education in response to the growing turn towards student-centred pedagogies (Lean et al. 2006). Teaching through games responds to the challenge of producing a more active body of students in a variety of ways (Ritzko and Robinson 2006). First by providing an immediate and intuitive entry into the topics. Second, by making learning a highly interactive process, through which students actively build their knowledge rather than being simply its 'consumers'. Third, by encouraging students to interact and collaborate with each other, gaming contributes to the socialising function of education and improves their social and communication skills.

The game in this chapter introduces students to key tenets of IR theories. It specifically allows students to understand how IR theories explain conflict

DOI: 10.4324/9781003230120-2

and cooperation between states. It also invites students to reflect on the role of theorising, whether it is about explaining the world or constituting it.

This game is especially useful for first-year students in politics and IR. It is a tool to provide them with an accessible entry into what could initially seem a distant and obscure topic. The use of this adapted version of the prisoner's dilemma supports students' engagement with the subject by connecting it to mechanisms of individual decision-making, which are more intuitive and easily relatable. The pedagogical logic behind this game is analogy. Analogies "allow students to understand a new concept or situation by seeing how it relates to (or is analogous to) a more familiar situation" (Pallas and Butcher 2017, 100–1). By creating this connection, analogies render the "unfamiliar familiar" (Duit 1991, 651). The prisoner's dilemma might have been encountered by students in other contexts, including popular culture such as TV programmes. Even if unfamiliar to some students, it is easy to explain and is intuitively grasped by most students. Through the use of "simple models of human behaviour" (Ehrhardt 2008, 58) the aim is to support students in understanding generalisable logics of how "individuals' decisions are interrelated and how those decisions result in outcomes" (Morrow 1994, 1).

This game introduces the key tenets of different IR theories in one session. This approach complements the more traditional approach of IR theory modules which often introduces one theory per session. Surely, in order to understand each of these theories in depth, it is necessary to dedicate specifically focused sessions to analyse each of those in detail. However, there are two specific advantages of a joint introduction to different IR theories through this game-based session. First, it offers a non-compartmentalised approach to IR theory. Rather than presenting each theory individually, this pedagogical approach promotes dialogue across different theories. This is important to enhance cross-fertilisation between different approaches, and it avoids disciplinary rigidity, which risks hindering "the task of analysing pressing issues in global politics" (Peoples and Vaughan-Williams 2015, 10). This is especially important since a theory alone struggles to capture the complexity of global politics (Ashley 1996) and the discipline has seen an increasing blurring of the lines between different IR theories and the co-fertilisation of different theoretical approaches to generate insights (Morgan 2003, 359). Second, in terms of transferable skills, this develops the ability of students to exercise problem-thinking as well as problem-solving skills in a multi-faceted and changing scenario. Exposing students to the plurality of the discipline from the very beginning pushes their own ability to choose and select different concepts, theories and beliefs and develops their own agency (Morgan 2003, 365).

After briefly illustrating the dilemma, the class is divided into small teams playing in pairs '*against and with*' one another. The educator probes teams to decide whether to cooperate or not. At each round of the game, the educator introduces variants in the roles, identities and structural conditions of the prisoners. After a brief consultation, the teams declare their decision simultaneously at the count of three. By reasoning on the outcomes and the assumptions underpinning their decisions, students explore the core tenets of different IR theories.

In reflecting on the outcomes at the end of the game, the lecturer will focus on two key aspects. First, to what extent did students feel that they were able to take the most rational decision, and to what extent as the game proceeded, did they feel that they were increasingly driven by their own emotions (desire for revenge for a previous decision, fear to be seen as too trustworthy by their peers, etc.). This allows us to reflect on the role of emotions in IR. Specifically to see emotions not as something that can be eliminated but as something that lies "at the very core of human existence" and therefore is part of our decision-making process (Hutchison 2018).

Second, students are asked to reflect on how their decisions were driven by their very theorising on how the other team would have behaved and by the information that they were given about them. Indeed, playing the prisoner's dilemma gives students a sense of "experienced subjectivity" (Morgan 2003; Ehrhardt 2008, 60), allowing students to explore the constitutive effects of the very act of 'playing'. This means that the educator can draw attention to the fact that it is the very students' practice of theorising on what their adversary would do that brings about actions, which then can be explained in terms of different theories. Additionally, the instructions given by the educator about their characters (partners in crime, then friends, then part of the same criminal syndicate, etc.) 'dictate' the way in which students see each other and guide their actions. These observations open a reflection on how "discourse", thus theory, is not simply "a way of learning 'about' something out there in the 'real world'; it is rather a way of producing that something as real, as identifiable, as classifiable, knowable and therefore, meaningful" (Klein 1987 in Grayson 2008, 15). This allows students to reflect on the function of theories, which is not only explanatory but also constitutive of the reality they seek to explain. From this perspective, theories are not detached and neutral but are part of the constitution they seek to understand. This means that this game cannot only be applied to teach IR theories informed by positivism and rational choice theory but can also be used to teach the key tenets of constructivist and critical theories.

Understanding key tenets of IR theory can be transferred to analysing different real-world scenarios, especially with regards to understanding the incentives and disincentives of actors to cooperate or not. This game can also be 'scaled down' to understand (international) conflict management, especially to assess motivations of individuals to engage in negotiation or to respect ceasefires. In sociology, this game can be transferred to consider motivations/incentives informing the choice of groups in a society to cooperate or not.

A workshop with educators will address three main aspects. First, educators will need to familiarise themselves with this adapted version of the prisoner's dilemma. Second, educators will have to play the game themselves. Third, they will need to discuss possibilities for debriefing students, especially with regard to the final reflection at the end of the game. It is also important to reflect on how the knowledge of each theory can be deepened in follow-up sessions. It is important to be aware that while the game provides an intuitive and engaging entry into IR theories, further exploration of each theory is required to deepen students' understanding of these. Additionally, the learning points of the game and the logic that they illuminate about international behaviour could be recalled in other lectures to discuss different real-world scenarios. As Ehrhardt argues, incorporating the logics of a game in lectures on a variety of topics makes games useful for student learning (2008, 58).

2.2 Games Details

2.2.1 Key Skills

IR theory, emotions and rationality, constitutive and explanatory approaches to theory.
　　Transferable Skills: analytical and self-reflexive, decision-making skills

2.2.2 Group Size

Learners working in teams. Ideally, each team is a small group of three to five learners. Team size can vary, but it needs to be small enough to allow students to speak to each other without the other team being able to hear what is discussed. Each team is paired with another team, and they play with and against each other. Ideally, there should not be more than three pairs of teams playing at the same time, to ensure that a single instructor can easily coordinate the game and give effective feedback.

2.2.3 Time

Ninety minutes or more. Timing can be flexible, depending on how many theories the educator aims at introducing.

2.2.4 Purpose (Learning Objectives)

1. To develop an understanding of the key tenets of different IR theories including Realism[1], Liberalism[2] and Constructivism[3].
2. To introduce the difference between explanatory and constitutive approaches to theory.
3. To reflect on the role of rationality and emotions in IR theories.
4. To reflect on decision-making patterns concerning cooperation and non-cooperation.

2.2.5 Preparation and Setup

- Room – The room requires two whiteboards, two papers per team and pens. Students need their notepads to take notes and solidify their learning.
- This game does not require any technological support.

2.2.6 Guidance

It is essential that the classroom is set up so that students can discuss secretively in their groups and reach their decision without being heard by the other team (see Figure 2.1). I usually give students instructions on how to arrange the room to play the game, prior to explaining it. I find that this supports creating a playful atmosphere and stimulates student curiosity.

As the game unfolds, students might be tempted to "bring the classroom dynamics into the game" and instead of deciding on the basis of the instructions, start to make decisions on the basis of what happened previously (for example, getting back at the other group for betraying them.) It is important to remind students to decide exclusively on the basis of the instructions. The role of their emotions in their decision-making process will be discussed in the final debrief.

Students might tend to decide on the basis of their previous knowledge of the prisoner's dilemma, which they acquired in other scenarios, including TV programmes, or previous academic studies (especially if they have a background in economics). It is important to stress from the beginning that they need to approach this game anew and discard prior knowledge.

Depending on the group of students, educators have two options. (1) they play the game until the end and then illustrate the analogies between the different scenarios and IR theories. (2) They interrupt the game with mini-debriefs to support students to connect each set of scenarios in the game with the corresponding IR theory. I found the latter option more effective in sustaining students' attention and understanding because it allowed me to illustrate how the game explains a specific IR theory while in-game decisions are still fresh in their minds. Additionally, these mini-debriefs give the opportunity to students to further explore their assumptions about their decisions.

It is important to urge students to take notes on the outcomes of the different rounds of the game and how these link to each theory under discussion. This will allow students to maintain their learning with concrete and easily accessible examples when each theory will be explored in more depth in follow-up sessions. When teaching a specific theory in depth in the follow-up session, it is useful to remind students of the specific scenario in the prisoner's dilemma game, as this supports their intuitive grasp of the theory.

The educator should be in charge of the countdown to make sure that teams communicate their decision at the same time. Selecting a student as a team leader per each group of players facilitates this.

2.2.7 Instructions

Table 2.1

A/B	Stay Silent (Cooperate)	Betray (Non-cooperate)
Stay Silent	1–1	4 (a)–0(b)
Betrays	0 (a)–4(b)	2–2

You are a thief who has been arrested by the police with your partner in crime. You are held in custody. You are placed in separate cells, and you cannot communicate with one another nor do you have access to a lawyer.

The police can prove that you are both guilty of stealing a car together. However, you also robbed a flat together. During the burglary, the flat owner fell down the stairs and sustained serious (although not lethal) injuries. The police suspect that both of you committed this major crime, but they do not have sufficient proof that it was you to convince a jury. For this reason, they are trying to pressure you to betray each other. They ask each of you to give them the necessary proof to accuse your partner in crime, and in exchange, they offer you a discount on the minor crime, which would allow you to avoid going to prison.

Thus, following Table 2.1 (on the whiteboard in the class), you each have the two following possibilities.

1) Decide to incriminate your partner by speaking to the police (non-cooperate, i.e. betray).
2) Decide to stay silent and not betray your partner by cooperating with your partner (cooperate).

Your decision can lead you to the following outcomes, depending on your partner's decision.

1) *You both cooperate with each other (i.e. you stay silent and do not speak to the police.) In this case, you are both sentenced for the minor crime only and you receive one year of prison each.*
2) *You both betray your partner. You are both incriminated for the minor crime and also share the responsibility for the major crime, receiving a sentence of two years in prison each.*
3) *One of you stays silent (cooperate) and one of you betrays (non-cooperate). In this case, the criminal who betrayed (non-cooperate) is absolved for the major crime and is pardoned for the minor crime and avoids a prison sentence. The criminal who did not betray (cooperate) is sentenced for both the minor and the major crimes and receives four years of prison.*

What will you do?

Figure 2.1 Classroom setup[4]

Arrange the classroom as shown in Figure 2.1.

Divide students into teams. There are three to five students on each team. On one side of the classroom, you will have all the prisoner 'A' teams and on the opposite side all the prisoner 'B' teams.

Explain to students the rationale for using this game as an analogy to introducing IR theories.

Read the brief outlined above to the students and explain the table while drawing it on a whiteboard.

Give two papers to each team and ask them to write with their pen 'cooperate' on one and 'betray' on the other.

For each team, assign one student as the 'team leader'. They will be in charge of showing the selected paper at the end of the countdown.

Double-check that the students understood the prisoner's dilemma. Asking students to explain it to their peers in their own words is an effective strategy.

Remind students of the key rules. (1) In-team discussions should be conducted quietly so that the other team cannot hear them. (2) They need to decide exclusively on the basis of the scenario and information provided by the educator, without making any other assumptions about the prisoners (e.g. identity, social and economic condition, personality, personal history).

For each round of decisions, give students two to three minutes to make their decision.

As the game proceeds, the educator will use the second whiteboard to show the analogies between the students' decisions in the game and key tenets of IR theories. (See Table 2.2 for the questions and key tenets of IR theories explored. This list is not exhaustive, and each educator would have the flexibility of modifying the scenario to explore additional theories.)

At the end of the game, the educator goes over what has been written on the whiteboard once more, which by now would include all the key tenets of the IR theories taken into consideration throughout the game and summarise it again by referring to what happened in the game. The last part of the session is a plenary debrief (questions).

Table 2.2 Possible IR scenarios and IR theories[5]

Scenario	Key Theories Learning Points	Notes
You are held in custody. You are placed in separate cells and you cannot communicate with one another nor do you have access to a lawyer.	*Realism:* Self-interest, self-reliance, lack of trust, survival, self-help	*At this point, students might ask questions to have more information about the specific character/social status of their criminal. This is an opportunity to reinstate other tenets of Structural Realism; "all states are alike" and the emphasis is on very generalisable similarities (see Morgan 2003, 357; Waltz 1979, 122).*

(Continued)

Table 2.2 (Continued) Possible IR scenarios and IR theories

Scenario	Key Theories Learning Points	Notes
Prisoner A finds a hidden message in their food from Prisoner B, promising that they will stay silent.	Realism/liberalism dilemma: Is human nature good or bad?	Students can discuss their assumptions about human nature, which drove their decision to trust or not to trust the other (or to respect their own pledge.) This also encourages debate on the role of communication.
You are business partners – you cannot do business without the other.	Liberalism: Economic interdependence increases possibilities of cooperation	
You both have mums waiting at home that would want to see you get the shortest time possible in prison.	Liberalism: Democratic peace theory – domestic context has a role in setting preferences of actors	
You both belong to a mafia syndicate that condemns treason.	Liberalism: Role of international organisations in setting incentives to cooperate	Students might raise questions about how powerful that mafia syndicate is, whether they can escape their justice and what ranks they have in the organisation. This helps explore the role of international organisations and how these might reflect existing hierarchies in the international system.
You are best friends.	Constructivism: The role of identity	Challenging Rationalist assumptions and the narrow focus on 'interests'
You have a long history of cooperating with each other/you have a long history of not cooperating.	Constructivism: Role of history in shaping states' behaviour and beliefs	
You have been taught that loyalty is the highest value.	Social Constructivism: Norms, standards of expected behaviours and institutions (logic of appropriateness)	This allows students to reflect on the role of 'socialisation'

(*Continued*)

Table 2.2 (Continued)   Possible IR scenarios and IR theories

Scenario	Key Theories Learning Points	Notes
You are siblings.	Transcend objectivist and positivist assumptions to help "students become acutely aware of their own beliefs, experience how these beliefs can interact with others in the creation of a common reality" (Morgan 2003, 361–2)	This scenario often gives mixed results. Students might motivate their decision on the basis of their personal relationships with their siblings. One student who was betrayed said "I hate my sister, I would never trust her". In this way, "students have the opportunity to begin to empathise, to understand, and to find meaning in contradictory points of view" (Morgan 2003, 364).
Further scenarios can attribute different identities, gender and socioeconomic conditions to the prisoners. For example, there might be a great disparity in wealth between the two (class), or/and one prisoner might be Black, Asian and minority ethnic and the other white (racial bias and institutional racism), or/and one prisoner might be a woman or lesbian, gay, bisexual, transgender and queer.	Marxism[6], Postcolonialism,[7] Feminism.[8] These theories expose overlooked assumptions of existing IR theories. This allows the lecturer to introduce how these factors are linked and intersect to influence outcomes in world politics. Examples include rich and poor states in the international system; racial bias and institutional racism; and self-reliance, individualism and constructions of masculinity at play in IR theories	Students can be invited to reflect on how these additional factors might affect their decision. At times, some students have mentioned that if the prisoners were two women, cooperation is more likely, as they are trustworthy. This can open up discussions about the very social construction of femininity and masculinity.

2.2.8 Debrief

Once the groups are back in plenary, the following debrief questions can be asked to get the participants to reflect on the exercise.

Do you think that this game will help you to remember the key tenets of the different IR theories? Can you name one key tenet for each theory?

Do you think that cooperation or conflict is more likely in contemporary global politics?

What roles did emotions have in your decision-making? Did emotions have an increasing/decreasing/stable importance in your decision-making process as the game was progressing?

Reflecting on your experience of playing the game, what does this tell you about the nature of theoretical knowledge? Is it detached from the real world, or is it part of its constitution?

2.3 Adaptation of Game to a Different Context

Within the discipline of IR, the prisoner's dilemma can be easily adapted to help students' understand different topics. For example, Ehrhardt includes "Security Dilemma, Arms Races, Nuclear Deterrence, Economic cartels, Tariffs Protection" (2008, 63). Others include the difficulties of the international community in addressing collective issues such as climate change. Equally this game can be used to explore regional issues, such as the (in)ability of Europe to cooperate on the migrant and refugee crisis. For each possible scenario, the instructor could choose to develop the theoretical aspects which are most relevant for that specific discipline.

Notes

1 "In the discipline of International Relations (IR), realism is a school of thought that emphasises the competitive and conflictual side of international relations. (…) The first assumption of realism is that the nation-state (usually abbreviated to 'state') is the principle actor in international relations. (…) Second, the state is a unitary actor. (…) Third, decision-makers are rational actors in the sense that rational decision-making leads to the pursuit of the national interest". Sandrina Antunes and Isabel Camisão "Realism", in *International Relations Theory*, edited by Stephen McGlinchey, Rosie Walters and Christian Scheinpflug E-IR: Bristol, 2017, p. 15.
2 "The basic insight of the theory [Liberalism]is that the national characteristics of individual States matter for their international relations. (…) Liberal theorists have often emphasized the unique behaviour of liberal States, though more recent work has sought to extend the theory to a general domestic characteristics-based explanation of international relations". Anne-Marie Slaughter "International Relations, Principal Theories", Princeton, 2011, p.14 available at https://scholar.princeton.edu/sites/default/files/slaughter/files/722_intlrelprincipaltheories_slaughter_20110509zg.pdf.
3 In the Constructivist account, the variables of interest to scholars – e.g. military power, trade relations, international institutions or domestic preferences – are not important because they are objective facts about the world, but rather because they have certain social meanings (Wendt 2000). This meaning is constructed from a complex and specific mix of history, ideas, norms and beliefs, which scholars must understand if they are to explain state behaviour. Anne-Marie Slaughter "International Relations, Principal Theories", Princeton, 2011, p.14 available at https://scholar.princeton.edu/sites/default/files/slaughter/files/722_intlrelprincipaltheories_slaughter_20110509zg.pdf, p. 19.
4 Illustration by Giulia Leonardi.
5 The borders between IR theories are not as neat, and often scholars use cross-fertilisation to produce insights. Therefore, for example, some tenets which I attribute to Social Constructivism might also inform Liberalism. Also, Realism has eschewed the radicalism of Waltz structural realism's understanding of states as an abstract unit of analysis to include, for example, insights from historical sociology especially on the role of historical context in shaping states' behaviour

(see, for example, Ayoob 2002). Therefore, the subdivision, which I use to play the game, is by no means the only possibility and must be understood as illustrative only.

6 "The work of Marxists is (…) to figure out how the capitalist mode of production and the sovereign states system emerged – as two sides of the same coin. (…) To explain Marxism in IR, we need to start with Marx's main theory for the development of capitalism: historical materialism. Most simply, historical materialism asserts that human beings – including their relations with each other and their environment – are determined by the material conditions in which they can survive and reproduce". Maïa Pal, "Marxism", in *International Relations Theory*, edited by Stephen McGlinchey, Rosie Walters and Christian Scheinpflug E-IR: Bristol, 2017, p. 43.

7 "The use of 'post' by postcolonial scholars by no means suggests that the effects or impacts of colonial rule are now long gone. Rather, it highlights the impact that colonial and imperial histories still have in shaping a colonial way of thinking about the world and how Western forms of knowledge and power marginalise the non-Western world". Sheila Nair, "Postcolonialism", in *International Relations Theory*, edited by Stephen McGlinchey, Rosie Walters and Christian Scheinpflug. Bristol: E-IR, 2017, p. 69.

8 "[F]eminist theory has shown that traditional IR is in fact gender-blind. Feminist scholarship therefore takes both women and gender seriously – and in doing so it challenges IR's foundational concepts and assumptions. (…) In making sense of IR in a way that takes both women and gender seriously, feminism has demonstrated the construction of gendered identities that perpetuate normative ideas of what men and women should do". Sarah Smith, "Feminism", in *International Relations Theory*, edited by Stephen McGlinchey, Rosie Walters and Christian Scheinpflug. Bristol: E-IR, 2017, pp. 62–3.

Bibliography

Ashley, R. (1996). The achievements of post-structuralism". In: S. Smith, K. Booth, and M. Zalewski, eds., *International theory: positivism and beyond*, Cambridge: Cambridge University Press, pp. 240–53.

Ayoob, M. (2002). Inequality and theorizing in international relations: the case for subaltern realism. *International Studies Review*, 4(3), pp. 27–48. Retrieved 28 October 2020, from http://www.jstor.org/stable/3186462

Duit, R. (1991). On the role of analogies and metaphors in learning science. *Science Education* 75(6), 649–72.

Ehrhardt, G. (2008). Beyond the prisoner's dilemma: making a useful part of undergraduate international relations classes. *International Studies Perspectives*, 9, pp. 57–74.

Grayson, G. (2008). Fine points on productive learning. *Physics Today*, 61(9), p. 15.

Hutchison, E. (2018). Why study emotions in international relations? E-IR [online], https://www.e-ir.info/2018/03/08/why-study-emotions-in-international-relations/

Keyle, G. (2008). *Chasing dragons: security, identity and illicit drugs in Canada*. Toronto: University of Toronto Press.

Klein, S.B. (1987). *Learning: principles and applications*. New York: McGraw-Hill Book Company.

Lean, J., Moizer, J., Towler, M., and Abbey, C. (2006). Simulations and games: use and barriers in higher education. *Active Learning in Higher Education*, 7(3), pp. 227–42.

McGlinchey, S., Walters, R., and Scheinpflug, C. (eds.). (2017). *International relations theory*. Bristol: E-IR.

Morgan, A. L. (2003). Toward a global theory of mind: the potential benefits of presenting a range of IR theories through active learning. *International Studies Perspectives*, 4, pp. 351–70.
Morrow, James D. (1994). *Game theory for political scientists*. Princeton: Princeton University Press.
Pallas, I Christopher and Butcher, Charity. (2017). Using dating as an analogy to teach IR theory. *European Political Science,* 16, pp. 99–112.
Peoples, C. and Vaughan-Williams, N. (2015). *Critical security studies: a critical introduction*. Routledge: London and New York.
Ritzko, J. M. and Robinson, S. (2006). Using games to increase active learning. *Journal of College Teaching & Learning (TLC)*, 3(6), pp. 45–50.
Slaughter, A.-M. (2011). *International relations, principal theories*. Princeton. Available at: https://scholar.princeton.edu/sites/default/files/slaughter/files/722_intlrelprincipaltheories_slaughter_20110509zg.pdf.
Waltz, K. (1979). *Theory of International Politics*. Boston, MA: McGraw-Hill.
Wendt, Alexander. (2000). A social theory of international politics. *Social Theory of International Politics*, 26. https:/doi.org/10.1017/CBO9780511612183

3 Using Role Play to Teach Learners How to Negotiate Using Different Strategies

Chandni Hirani

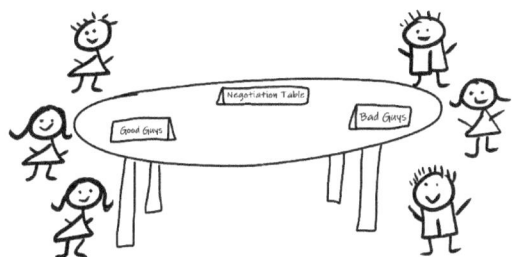

3.1 Overview

This game introduces students to the concepts of distributive[1] and integrative[2] negotiations. The intention is to provide students with the opportunity to discover the nature of these two types of negotiations through role play. Learning through play is an effective way to learn a skill, and role play enables students to step into a persona and practically participate in the skills-building activity. This form of active learning enables the learners to better conceptualise, which in turn results in a deeper learning (Kilgour et al. 2015). Active learning is further defined as a learning approach that results in immediate reflection on the concepts being taught. By role-playing negotiation scenarios, students can begin to get a sense of their own negotiation personas. Reflection should lead to self-awareness of their negotiation skills gap. The overall objective of this activity is to enable students to remember this skill going forward due to the engaging nature of active role play. This can be achieved as the role-play activity is complex enough to allow the learner to engage with the skill long enough to substantially practice it (Hess 2007).

This game is inspired by the employment negotiation role-play simulation developed by the Program on Negotiation at the Harvard Law School, as well as the Negotiation Analysis Course at the London School of Economics. In this game, students will engage in a two-person negotiation where a new company recruit will negotiate their terms of employment with their new employer.

DOI: 10.4324/9781003230120-3

This scenario has been chosen as it is one of the most common types of negotiations that students are likely to engage in during their careers from both the perspective of employee and employer. Additionally, teaching leadership skills is necessary to set up the learners for leadership roles in the future. Being an employer who is negotiating an employee's salary can be both difficult and uncomfortable, therefore this activity allows the learners to engage with this skill in a safe environment (Kilgour et al. 2015). Whilst not all parts of the negotiation reflect a real employer-employee negotiation, the purpose is to provide a scenario where the maximum amount of learning can be achieved.

This game is intended for students who have little or no knowledge of the concepts of distributive or integrative negotiations. However, it can be adapted for students with some experience in negotiations by developing more complex negotiation scenarios such as multi-party negotiations. The game outlines three different scenario simulations: distributive, integrative and optional (participants choose which of the strategies to adopt). The intention is to have different pairs of students role-playing these simulations to demonstrate the impact they each have on negotiation outcomes.

In addition to this being a useful learning tool for students, it can be used as a valuable teaching tool, enabling educators to upskill themselves on the effectiveness of role-play simulations. Role play as a mode of active learning has been widely used in teacher education, as the realistic nature of the learning helps future teachers better understand concepts through this deep learning (Neuendorf and O'Connell 2011). By engaging in the role-play activity themselves, educators can get an appreciation of the nature of these negotiations by debriefing the activity from the perspective of both learner and educator.

3.2 Games Details

3.2.1 Key Skills

Integrative negotiation, distributive negotiation, communication, hiring

3.2.2 Group Size

Any even number – learners working in pairs

3.2.3 Time

1 hour 15 minutes – inclusive of role play activity and debrief

3.2.4 Purpose (Learning Objectives)

1. To develop an understanding of the differences between integrative and distributive negotiation strategies
2. To improve communication skills through the practical exercise of a negotiation

3.2.5 Preparation and Setup

For 24 students print:

- 12 copies of Material 1
- 12 copies of Material 2
- 4 copies of Material 3
- 4 copies of Material 4
- 4 copies of Material 5

3.2.6 Instructions

Students will be engaging in a role-play activity to learn the difference between integrative and distributive negotiations. The purpose of a distributive negotiation is to achieve gains only for yourself i.e., an 'all or nothing' scenario. The objective of an integrative negotiation is to achieve mutual gains – i.e., a 'win-win' scenario. This involves every party at the bargaining table positively gaining from the negotiation.

<u>Scenario Brief:</u> The **scenario** in this activity is a negotiation between ***a company recruiter and a new hire***. The new hire has already passed through the interview stage, and this negotiation is to determine the terms of employment. Each student will be assigned a role to play, as well as a scenario to play. There are only two roles (company recruiter, new hire) and three scenario simulations (distributive, integrative, optional). Students should not share details of their role and scenario with anyone else. Students will be given a fixed amount of time to role-play the negotiation. At the end of this time, students will reconvene in a plenary to have a debrief and share the outcomes of their individual negotiations. A non-agreement is a valid outcome for this activity and will be discussed in the debrief.

Read the brief outlined above to the students.

Divide students into pairs (e.g. if there are 24 students, there should be 12 pairs).

For each pair, assign one student as the "company recruiter" and one student as the "new hire".

Give every "company recruiter" material 1 from the handouts and give every "new hire" material 2 from the handouts.

STUDENTS MUST NOT SHARE THEIR HANDOUT MATERIAL WITH THE OTHER PERSON IN THEIR PAIR.

There are four areas that need to be negotiated: "salary", "location", "annual bonus" and "annual leave".

The objective is to aim for a settlement closest to the highest points for each of the four areas.

Assign each pair one of the three scenarios in the handouts. Ensure the three scenarios are evenly distributed among the group (e.g. if there are 12 pairs, there will be 4 pairs assigned to each scenario).

For every pair assigned to scenario 1, give material 3.1 only to the person playing the role of "company recruiter" and give material 3.2 only to the person playing the role of "new hire". Repeat this with the appropriate material to the pairs assigned to scenarios 2 and 3

STUDENTS MUST NOT SHARE THEIR HANDOUT MATERIAL WITH THE OTHER PERSON IN THEIR PAIR.

Give the students ten minutes to look over the handout materials they have – each person should have two materials to review (role, scenario) and should not share their material with anyone. They should develop their negotiation strategy based on the material they have been given.

Give the students 20 minutes to conduct the negotiation by playing the roles they have been assigned.

Once students have concluded their negotiation, they should record on a piece of paper the outcome of their negotiation and the terms of agreement or disagreement.

Students will gather in a plenary to share outcomes of their negotiations and debrief as a group for 20 minutes.

3.2.7 Guidance

Students may be tempted to look at each other's handout materials – please ensure they do not do this in order to have the most effective negotiation experience and outcomes.

There is no right answer to the negotiations nor is there any "winner" – the objective is to learn about the different approaches used in negotiations and reflect on them.

The points structure in the handouts is to indicate to the students what is in the best interests of their assigned role – they should therefore aim to negotiate at the higher end of their point structure.

"Location" has the same point structure for both roles – this is to highlight that sometimes both parties have the same interests.

The purpose of scenario 1 is to test the distributive negotiation strategy – there should be a higher rate of "no deals" or a higher rate of dissatisfied parties with the agreed-upon deals.

The purpose of scenario 2 is to test the integrative negotiation strategy – there should be a higher rate of "deals" and a higher rate of satisfied parties with the agreed-upon deals.

The purpose of scenario 3 is to allow individual students to choose their own negotiation strategy and see how many choose the distributive approach and how many choose the integrative approach. This may therefore involve different strategies on opposite sides of the same negotiation, so students should not tell their partners what strategy they are selecting before starting.

3.2.8 Debrief

Once the groups are back in plenary, the following debrief questions can be asked to get the participants to reflect on the exercise.

Using Role Play to Teach Learners 29

What were the terms of your negotiation agreement?
Were there any pairs that didn't come to an agreement?
What were the different outcomes of the negotiations based on the different scenarios assigned?
Is there a pattern we can identify for the outcomes based on these scenarios?
Did scenario 1 result in more 'no terms agreed' situations?
Did scenario 2 result in more 'terms agreed' situations?
What kind of results did scenario 3 present?
Did scenario 2 demonstrate the 'win-win' strategy at play?
What have we learnt about the three different scenarios and the outcomes of the negotiations?
How would I negotiate differently if I were to do this again without an assigned scenario?
What have we learnt about 'win-win'/integrative negotiating and 'fixed'/distributive negotiating?
How do we think we can transfer this skill of negotiating to a different context?
Do we think learning this skill through role play was a beneficial and engaging way to learn?

Examples of negotiation issues that participants can introduce to make an integrative negotiation include the following:

- *Parental leave*
- *Remote work/flexible work*
- *Job title*
- *Travel reimbursement*
- *Children's school fees bursary*
- *Professional development bursary*

3.2.9 Handouts and Material

Material 1:		*Additional Information for <u>COMPANY RECRUITER</u>*					
Salary		**Location**		**Annual bonus**		**Annual leave**	
	Points		Points		Points		Points
20,000 USD	9	London	6	100 USD	6	10 days	3
25,000 USD	6	Nairobi	4	200 USD	4	15 days	2
30,000 USD	3	Abuja	2	300 USD	2	20 days	1
35,000 USD	0	Lisbon	0	400 USD	0	25 days	0

Copyright material from Hirani & Varin 2003, *Supporting Adult Learners through Games and Interactive Teaching*, Routledge

Material 2:		Additional Information for <u>NEW HIRE</u>					
Salary		**Location**		**Annual bonus**		**Annual leave**	
	Points		Points		Points		Points
20,000 USD	0	London	6	100 USD	0	10 days	0
25,000 USD	3	Nairobi	4	200 USD	2	15 days	1
30,000 USD	6	Abuja	2	300 USD	4	20 days	2
35,000 USD	9	Lisbon	0	400 USD	6	25 days	3

Material 3.1:   SCENARIO 1 Negotiation Strategy for <u>COMPANY RECRUITER</u>:
Very fixed and hard approach, not willing to give much to the new hire

Material 3.2:   SCENARIO 1 Negotiation Strategy for <u>NEW HIRE</u>:
Very fixed and hard approach, not willing to give much to the recruiter

Material 4.1:   SCENARIO 2 Negotiation Strategy for <u>COMPANY RECRUITER</u>:
Willing to be reasonable by introducing other benefits into the negotiation to make it more appealing – e.g. maternity/paternity leave, flexible working hours, insurance

Material 4.2:   SCENARIO 2 Negotiation Strategy for <u>NEW HIRE</u>:
Willing to meet the company recruiter halfway if she/he is reasonable and adds extra benefits. Suggest a range of benefits to the recruiter

Material 5.1:   SCENARIO 3 Negotiation Strategy for <u>COMPANY RECRUITER</u>:
Develop your own negotiation strategy – e.g. hard negotiator, reasonable negotiator, creative negotiator – by introducing other benefits

Material 5.2:   SCENARIO 3 Negotiation Strategy for <u>NEW HIRE</u>:
Develop your own negotiation strategy – e.g. hard negotiator, reasonable negotiator, creative negotiator – by introducing other benefits

3.3 Adaptation of the Games to a Different Context

Role plays to demonstrate negotiations in various different settings are simple to set up. The following are three types of negotiations that can be developed:

- *A business negotiation*

A B2B[3] or B2C[4] relationship between a supplier and buyer can be played out in a negotiation where a buyer can be negotiating the price of a product

Copyright material from Hirani & Varin 2003, *Supporting Adult Learners through Games and Interactive Teaching*, Routledge

with a supplier. This is a particularly useful negotiation scenario for business students.

- *A multi-party negotiation*

A three- or four-person negotiation can be set up between a private investor, government entity and local community to determine the outcomes of a new infrastructure project (e.g. a new mining project in a rural community). This is particularly useful to teach the concepts of coalition building. This scenario would be beneficial for development and international relations students. The scenario can be changed to buying a company to suit business students.

- *A real-life political negotiation*

The Brexit negotiations between the UK government and the European Union to demonstrate the complexity of some negotiations and to highlight the impact different types of negotiator personalities make on a negotiation.

Notes

1. Distributive negotiation is a bargaining strategy also referred to as 'zero-sum', 'win-lose' or 'slicing the pie'. The intention of a distributive negotiation is for one party to gain with the opposing party losing. Distributive bargaining will leave one party unsatisfied with the outcome of the negotiation. Competitive negotiation.
2. Integrative negotiation is a bargaining strategy also referred to as 'win-win' or 'expanding the pie'. The intention of an integrative negotiation is for both parties to walk away from the negotiation table gaining positively. It requires collaboration to reach an outcome where both sides gain at the end of the negotiation. Collaborative negotiation.
3. B2B refers to a Business-to-Business relationship where commercial transactions between businesses are made.
4. B2C refers to a Business-to-Consumer relationship where a business sells a product or service directly to the customer.

Bibliography

Hess, P. (2007). Enhancing leadership skill development by creating practice/feedback opportunities in the classroom. *Journal of Management Education*, 31, p. 195.

Kilgour, P., Reynaud, D., Northcote, M. T. and Shields, M. (2015). Role-playing as a tool to facilitate learning, self-reflection and social awareness in teacher education. *International Journal of Innovative Interdisciplinary Research*, 2(4), pp. 8–20.

Michael, J. (2006). Where's the evidence that active learning works? *Advances in Physiology Education*, 30(4), pp. 159–67.

Neuendorf, P. and O'Connell, M. (2011). To be or not to be? That is the role play question. In: M. J. Koehler and P. Mishra (eds.), *Proceedings of the Society for Information Technology & Teacher Education International Conference*. Nashville, Tennessee: Society for Information Technology & Teacher Education.

4 Toffeconomy

Creating a Fictional Society to Illustrate Economic Concepts

Rudi Ackerman

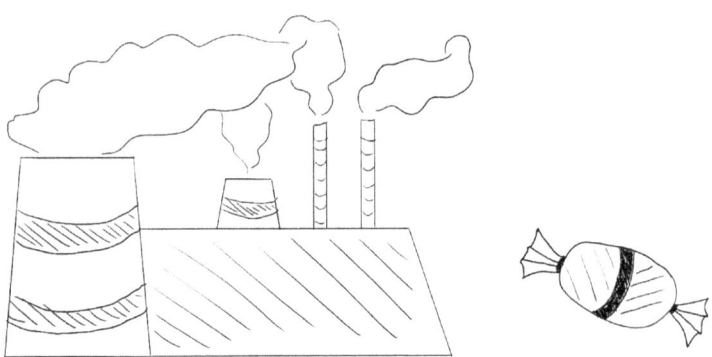

4.1 Overview

This is a game that teaches macroeconomic concepts related to fiscal and monetary policy. Using a game to teach these abstract concepts makes it much easier for students to understand and conceptualise how this will work in reality. Pivec et al. (2003) explain how in game-based learning settings, learners are naturally encouraged to combine knowledge from different areas when making choices. This makes game-based learning especially well-suited to economic learning since economics is predicated on the concept of combining various knowledge-sets (politics, sociology, mathematics, probability, etc.). In addition, Pivec et al. (2003) also point out the inherent social aspect that exists in game-based learning which helps students benefit from peer-to-peer learning. This social aspect also allows the instructor to better balance the often cold, utilitarian aspects prevalent in economic literature with the fun, lived experience of a social classroom-based game. Simply talking about a concept like the fallacy of composition in economics can leave students disinterested and sceptical. But playing a game that shows students how their very own choices cause the fallacy of composition is a much more powerful learning experience.

Tobias and Fletcher (2014) also talk about the impact that game-based learning has on student motivation. They find that introducing game-based aspects into the learning environment dramatically increases student

DOI: 10.4324/9781003230120-4

engagement. Banfield and Wilkerson (2014) also found gamification increased both intrinsic self-motivation and self-efficacy. In a field that is notorious for low student motivation, using games effectively can make an incredible difference. Students are often disengaged because the concepts in an economics class are complex and large, requiring significant motivation on the side of the student. Games are an effective way to self-start this motivation process by breaking down these complex concepts into fun, engaging learning challenges.

Plass et al. (2015) mention four main aspects of effective game-based learning. The game should be cognitive, affective, motivational and sociocultural. Using candy (in this case toffees) as a play tool invests students in the outcomes and allows them to experience similar incentives as we would see in the real economy. This helps make the game effective and motivational since students compete for instant gratification. It also makes it more fun and increases engagement levels as students get more and more passionate about buying toffee. The fact that bidding takes place in plenary with students often banding together to form conglomerates, makes this game sociocultural. Finally, the consistent discussion and interspersal of explanations by the lecturer after each round of bidding makes the game cognitive.

The game simulates a basic autarky[1] economy with a single product, a domestic auction trading mechanism and limited government intervention. It can illustrate the dynamics of money supply and demand in the economy and the effect of an increase in production vs. the increase in money supply (quantitative easing). It may be especially useful as a tool to help illustrate the IS-LM Model or the AS-AD Model[2] in macroeconomics, but it is not necessary that these curves be understood before playing this game. The game's basic setup can be altered to show other macroeconomic effects as well.

For educators, this game could serve as an example of how complex concepts can be explained using simple game dynamics. Other examples of this are the games developed by Jacob Clifford[3] who, among other things, adapted Vernon Smith's supply and demand experiment into a learning game.

4.2 Games Details

4.2.1 Key Skills

Monetary policy, fiscal policy, inflation, money supply and demand

4.2.2 Group Size

25–35 students

4.2.3 Time

1 hour (plus 30 minutes for debriefing)

4.2.4 Purpose (Learning Objectives)

1. To illustrate the effect of monetary and fiscal policy on the macroeconomy
2. To illustrate what happens with the value of money when changing the supply and demand of money in an economy

4.2.5 Preparation and Setup

- At least 50 toffees/candy pieces
- At least 150 currency items (you can use monopoly money, printed pieces of paper, a Post-it note folded in half so that it sticks to itself and makes a rectangle or any other item that students cannot easily duplicate)
- This game does not require any technological support

4.2.6 Instructions

Students are told the following scenario and then go through a series of bidding rounds, with the educator acting as the auctioneer. The currency used in the scenario is the dollar.

You are all citizens of Toffeconomy, a nation built upon the toffee industry. Every year, the country's single toffee factory produces a toffee that you can all bid on in a free market auction. The highest bidder gets the toffee. Everyone starts off with their basic salary, which is $1. After each bid is concluded, make sure to collect the currency from the group so that it can be used in subsequent rounds.

Read the brief outlined above to the students.

Give each student $1 of the currency item you will be using.

ROUND 1: Show students the toffee, and ask for opening bids. In auctioneer fashion, bids can be accepted by saying, "Going once, going twice and SOLD!" This gives students time to outbid each other and build tension.

After round 1, note on a blackboard the final price of the toffee.

ROUND 2: Give each student their normal salary of $1, and resume bidding the same as round 1.

Again, note the final price of the toffee. The price often comes to roughly double the price of the first toffee – indicating that 100% inflation has now occurred because 100% increase in money supply has happened. This may be distorted by the formation of student conglomerates, which may mean a much higher price is found.

ROUND 3: Explain that in this year, a populist leader was elected on the maxim of "Toffee for all!" and decided to print more money (you can use a slogan that invokes a populist leader's maxim in your geography and time. For example, if you are in South Africa around the 2010s, you might use the image of Julius Malema and the maxim "Pay Back the Money!"). In this round, each student receives an additional $1 as welfare from the state – coming to a total of $2 income in this round.

Again, note the final price of the toffee. This round, the price will be significantly higher than before. Point out to students that just because everyone has more money, does not mean people are better off – there is still only one toffee, and its price has increased because money supply has increased. This is inflation.

ROUND 4: In this year, a leader was elected that promised to industrialise the economy and invest in infrastructure and industry. Students do not get their income this year, and everyone with more than $10 needs to pay the rest in wealth tax. The leader builds an additional toffee factory. This year, two toffees are auctioned individually, one after the other.

Note down the price for both of the toffees. The price would be significantly lower than before and is indicative of the fact that money supply remained constant but production increased. If you have previously introduced students to the IS-LM curve, this can be used to show the effect of prices when production increases but money supply remains constant.

ROUND 5: This year, income of $1 gets distributed, and two toffees are produced. Again, note the price after the auction. It should be slightly higher than the previous year, showing the effect of an increase in money supply.

ROUND 6: This year, another factory is built, but the income is not taxed. A total of three toffees are sold, and each student gets an income of $1. Again, note the price; it should be closer to the previous price or only slightly higher, showing what happens when both money supply and productivity increase.

ROUND 7: Mention that this is the final year and that in this year, two of the factories burnt down because of terrorist activity, so only one toffee will be sold, while income remains the same at $1. Note the price afterwards; it should be significantly higher than before since there was a large drop in productivity as well as desperation and panic in the market (being the last round). Explain that this is the reason why we often see hyper-inflation in times of civil difficulty, wars or uncertainty.

4.2.7 Debrief

Once the groups are back in plenary, the following debrief questions can be asked to get the participants to reflect on the exercise.

Before coming into this class, what value would you have given this currency item? In itself, it holds no value, and yet you all became quite passionate about owning as many of these as possible. Do you think the currency bills we use in real life also lack intrinsic value? If so, who gives it value? Consumers? Producers? The government?

We saw that simply printing money and giving it to everyone was not effective at making everyone better off. What alternatives could we have done instead?

Was wealth taxation popular? Was it needed? Would you have voted for it to be implemented if you could? How else could the government have done it?

Did the imposition of a wealth tax make you scared to show your wealth? Did you try to hide it after the wealth tax was imposed? In what ways can the government ensure that people don't evade taxes?

4.2.8 Guidance and Variants

Using relevant political figures in the news to contextualise the policies being implemented is useful to draw connections to reality. For example, when implementing the social welfare grant to everyone through an increase in money supply, South African students may resonate with a picture of Julius Malema having been now elected for the Toffeconomy on the maxim of "Take Back the Toffee!", or in the USA, a picture of Trump promising to "Make Toffee Great Again!" This helps students draw connections between real-world policies and the policies used in the game.

It may be a good idea to keep some toffees/candy in reserve so that after the final round, anyone can buy a toffee at the last market price without having to bid.

A very important component in the bidding is the expectations students have. After the first round, students may expect things to continue in a certain way and would act accordingly. The repetitive nature of rounds 4–6 is explicitly designed to create such a fixed expectation. It is therefore important that the educator not give away potential future rounds by foreshadowing or alluding to what may happen in the future. If the educator alludes to certain policies or changes in the future, students may decide to 'save' instead of participating, which would skew prices.

Students often may pool their money together and form ever-larger conglomerates to outbid others. This does not destroy the heuristic effect of the game and can even be the subject of discussion in the debriefing to help explain the value of corporate firms in an economy and the economies of scale this represents (as well as other firms' ability to compete). If you especially want this dynamic to form, it can be encouraged by arranging students on tables before the game begins so that conglomerates form naturally of varying sizes without necessarily dividing students into groups. However, the formation and changes within these conglomerates may cause some distortion to prices, which should be taken into account when debriefing each round.

Some ideas for variant rounds:

NATIONALISATION: You can insert an additional round between three and four (when groups are generally cash flush) where the government takes money from everyone and gives only their normal $2 salaries. This variant allows for fairer gameplay if you see large conglomerates forming that dominate smaller groups. It may also be used to illustrate the market panic that may happen with nationalisation policies.

CORPORATE INVESTMENT: In round 4, you can ask students to buy a factory instead of the government taxing everyone to build one. Students could buy a factory for $40 and would then receive one toffee that they must bid on and receive the income for it. This can also be done in round 6 where an additional factory is built. Then in round 7, the government factory can burn down, allowing wealth to be highly concentrated in the hands of the factory owners. This can be used as an illustration of the benefits and drawbacks of corporatisation.

Notes

1 "*Autarky*" refers to an economic state of being self-sufficient and unreliant on foreign trade or interventions. In this game, it implies that the country does not trade with any other countries and is, for all intents and purposes, the only country in the world.
2 The IS-LM Model (or Hicks-Hansen Model) is a macroeconomic staple often used to show the relationship between investment and savings (IS) and the liquidity and money supply (LM) in an economy. It is used as an auxiliary model in the AS-AD Model (or Aggregate Supply and Aggregate Demand Model), which shows macroeconomic supply and demand as a function of price levels and output. The models are based upon Keynesian and post-Keynesian economic thought.
3 For more on Jacob Clifford's games like the Handshake Market, the Pearl Exchange and others, follow his channel at https://www.youtube.com/user/ACDC Leadership

Bibliography

Banfield, J. and Wilkerson, B. (2014). Increasing student intrinsic motivation and self-efficacy through gamification pedagogy. *Contemporary Issues in Education Research (CIER)*, 7(4), pp. 291–8.

Pivec, M., Dziabenko, O. and Schinnerl, I. (2003). Aspects of game-based learning. In: *Proceedings of I-KNOW '03, 2003*, Graz, Austria (pp. 216–25).

Plass, J.L., Homer, B.D. and Kinzer, C.K. (2015). Foundations of game-based learning. *Educational Psychologist*, 50(4), pp. 258–83.

Spector, J. M. et al. (eds.) (2014). *Handbook of research on educational communications and technology*. New York: Springer Science+Business Media. https://doi.org/10.1007/978-1-4614-3185-5_38

Tobias, S., Fletcher, J.D. and Wind, A.P. (2014). Game-based learning. *Handbook of research on educational communications and technology*, pp. 485–503.

5 Pandemics, Popular Culture and Problem-Based Gaming
Teaching State Responses to Disease Control the 'Undead Way'

Malte Riemann

5.1 Overview

To understand state responses to pandemics/epidemics and their national and international implications.

Subject-matter skills: This session has three interrelated aims. First, to identify the security implications of pandemics. Second, to apply theoretical knowledge of international relations (IR) theories to the security dimensions of pandemics. Third, to identify and critically evaluate possible responses to a pandemic outbreak.

Transferable skills: (International) crisis management; analysis of open-ended, ill-structured problems; problem-solving skills.

This simulation game utilises a problem-based learning approach to games-based learning to teach crisis management skills and state responses to pandemics. Simulation gaming as a tool for teaching skills related to crisis management has been chosen because it allows for the construction of a complex learner-controlled learning that combines theory and practice in a realistic but risk-free learning environment (Salminen-Tuomaala and Koskela 2020). That simulation exercises are a beneficial learning tool has been widely noted (Shellman and Turan 2006; Wolf and Luethge 2003). Simulations offer the following advantages in achieving both the subject-matter skills intended for these sessions and the transferable skills to be developed:

First, simulation games can become sites for individual transformation that allows students to adopt the role of practitioners and policymakers (Clark et al. 2015; Shaffer 2006). This enables students to learn and practice novel ways of doing and being (Gaydos and Devane 2019). By adopting a role, simulation gaming encourages students to experiment and consider a variety of options, while simultaneously requiring them to engage in the setting of goals and the formulation of responses and strategies.

Second, simulations support lecture and theory validation through real-life application. Indeed, as Burke and Moore (2003) show, simulations go beyond traditional class activities and therefore are likely to stimulate better understanding of course content and narrow the gap between a complex reality and the classroom (Doyle and Brown 2000).

Third, as an active learning experience that promotes experiential learning, simulations allow for student attention to remain high. Compared to a traditional lecture or a lecture-style seminar, an active approach to teaching and learning, as the literature has shown, increases the likelihood of students maintaining attention. Furthermore, simulation games, as an experiential learning tool, encourage higher-order learning, promote critical thinking abilities and have shown themselves to be effective in facilitating self-directed learning (Kreber 2001). Simulations have shown themselves to be a specifically effective tool for teaching abstract concepts and theories (McCarthy 2014), and for this reason, they are an ideal teaching tool for introducing students to IR theories (Horn et al. 2016).

Furthermore, in order to enhance attention, I decided to infuse the use of a simulation game with a popular culture approach to teaching. Specifically, because the use of popular culture in the classroom is a good vehicle to address students with different educational backgrounds. As noted by Blanton,

> Bringing popular culture into the classroom can be very useful, particularly when teaching to non-majors who may have little or no background knowledge of global affairs, as it provides students with a familiar "anchor" through which to better understand core issues and concepts within IR.
>
> (Blanton 2012, 2)

To teach the security implications of pandemics, I chose a zombie invasion scenario as my popular culture trope. This choice was made for two reasons. First, zombies provide a good pop-cultural vehicle to address public health security concerns, as the lessons to be learnt from a zombie outbreak scenario are just as applicable as those from a real-world pandemic. Second, zombies are increasingly used to teach students about IR theories since the publication of *Theories of International Relations and Zombies* (Drezner 2011), which I used as a guide for this session. For these reasons, zombies allow this simulation to achieve three intended learning outcomes. In addition to these learning outcomes, zombies allow students, firstly, to scale down abstract concepts and theories to the level of a familiar pop-cultural trope; secondly, to enhance their learning outcomes through the use of a familiar narrative helping them to remember information more easily, and lastly, as students are used to talking about pop-cultural tropes outside the classroom, the use of the zombie narrative makes students more comfortable engaging in classroom activities (Blanton 2012).

The skills being taught are transferable to multiple crisis scenarios and crisis management situations in which units react to crises. For example, educators can replace the zombie scenario with a natural disaster scenario (e.g., a Tsunami affecting a region), with an environmental politics scenario (a resource crisis) or with an economic scenario (a sudden global economic collapse).

This game can be adapted by changing the scenario (e.g., by replacing zombies with a climate change scenario, see Section 5.3) and by changing the IR theories used (e.g., replacing Realism/Idealism with Constructivism/Feminism).

Additionally, educators could organise a 90- to 120-minute professional development session in which they take part in the zombie outbreak simulation themselves. This will allow educators to participate in the activity, provide each other with feedback on the simulation, share best practices and exchange ideas for how to improve the simulation/adapt the simulation to other contexts.

5.2 Games Details

Figure 5.1 shows the classroom setup.

5.2.1 Key Skills

(International) crisis management, IR theory, problem-solving skills

5.2.2 Group Size

This game is intended for small groups (ca. 12–20 learners) – learners are divided into four groups

5.2.3 Time

90 minutes

Pandemics, Popular Culture and Gaming 41

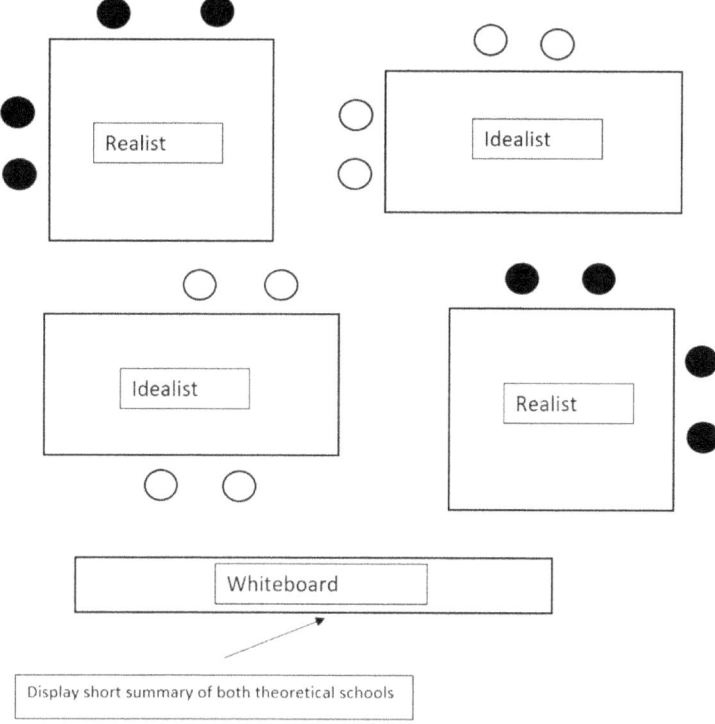

Figure 5.1 Classroom setup.

5.2.4 *Purpose (Learning Objectives)*

1. To identify the security implications of pandemics
2. To develop an understanding of state responses to pandemics/epidemics and their national and international implications
3. To consolidate knowledge of two IR theories (Idealism and Realism)

5.2.5 *Preparation and Setup*

- Room – Tables in the room need to be separated to create four collaborative spaces for the intended small group exercise to maximise students' communication during the group work. A whiteboard/large paper where the educator, after a brief revision discussion with the learners, writes down the key facets of the IR theories to be utilised in the exercise. Although not necessary, I felt that the exercise improved when students were provided with pens and a large sheet of paper to create a visual representation of their pandemic response.
- Tech – This exercise does not necessitate technology. However, to create a more immersive atmosphere, I displayed a PowerPoint with zombie

pictures on a wall and played fitting music (zombie film music throughout and Michael Jackson's hit song "Thriller" to conclude the exercise) in the background to create a relaxed atmosphere.

5.2.6 Guidance

Students may lack some familiarity with the IR theories used. For this reason, the instructor should use the first part of the session to review these together with the students and write the core tenets of these approaches onto a whiteboard.

On some occasions, it might prove effective to ask students about the potential security implications of pandemics prior to the simulation and to collect answers on a whiteboard. This could provide students with empirical material and food for thought for the following simulation exercise and to evaluate their engagement with possible pre-reading material.

Sometimes students might ask about the "nature" of the zombies (slow, fast, etc.), which should jointly be agreed upon.

The purpose of the scenario is the evaluation of IR theories, as well as the possible security implications of pandemics. For this reason, it is important to encourage students to make their responses applicable to the "real world" despite the fictional scenario.

Students can become competitive and see the simulation as a game with winners and losers. It is important that the educator clearly communicates that this simulation exercise will not have winners or losers but should be understood as a crisis mitigation exercise that places emphasis on the sharing of ideas instead of playful competition.

5.2.7 Instructions

The **scenario** in this activity is a fictional zombie pandemic outbreak.

Scenario:

> A zombie-virus outbreak has occurred, and the infection is rapidly spreading.
> You are in charge of drafting a state's response to this outbreak, taking both domestic and international responses into account.
> Your state has not yet been affected by this outbreak.

Scenario objectives:

- Identify domestic vulnerabilities and international objectives/interests.
- Establish responses across three domestic trajectories (social, economic, military) based on the vulnerabilities identified.
- Establish an international response based on the international objectives/interests set and the IR theory given.

Students are divided into four groups. Each group will be given a specific IR theory (two groups will use Realism and two use Idealism) along which the groups should frame their response. All four groups are asked to provide a state-based response to a zombie apocalypse, that, first, takes into account internal state measures along three trajectories (societal, economic, military), and, secondly, evaluates the international implications of a zombie invasion by evaluating how a state would react according to two IR theories (Realism/Idealism). A specific state will be chosen that all students will use in drafting their response to the scenario (e.g., the United Kingdom). This state has not yet been affected by the outbreak. Students will be given a fixed amount of time to develop their response. At the end of this time, students will reconvene in a plenary to have a debrief and share the responses their four groups have developed and compare and contrast these. After this discussion, students will leave the fictional zombie scenario and evaluate the groups' different responses in relation to contemporary pandemics like COVID-19, HIV/AIDS, Ebola and the Flu to establish a link between this fictitious scenario and real-world events.

Review in conjunction with the students the two theories chosen: Realism and Idealism (for a guide, see Table 5.1).

Introduce students to the fictional scenario.

Divide students into four groups. If there are 20 students, there should be 4 groups of 5 students. As this is a small group game, the maximum size for groups is seven students to allow each individual enough time to contribute to the group's response.

Two groups will be assigned to be 'Realists' and two groups will be 'Idealists'.

Students will address both domestic considerations and international considerations in their response.

The international response will be in line with the IR theory chosen for the group and should form a non-structured response to allow students the necessary space to think for themselves.

The domestic issues will be addressed following a structural outline. There are three domestic issues that students will need to address in their response: societal, economic and military.

The objective is to aim for a realistic response to the fictional zombie pandemic scenario.

Give the students 20 minutes to develop their responses.

While developing their responses, students should write the key steps their responses take on a piece of paper (encourage students to be creative and use visualisations such as maps or other images).

Once the 30 minutes are up, the four different groups will share their responses with the class.

The entire class will compare and contrast each other's approaches, identify differences and similarities, evaluate the validity of the different responses and whether or not these were in line with the theory chosen (i.e., Realism or Idealism). This can best be achieved by merging two groups at a time.

After this discussion, the class will leave the simulation game and evaluate the groups' different responses in relation to contemporary pandemics like COVID 19, HIV/AIDS, Ebola and the Flu.

Table 5.1 Brief Summary of Some Core Tenets in Realism and Idealism

	Realism	**Idealism**
Key Actors	States are the only actors at the international level.	States are not the sole actors. Other actors also play an important role. For example, international organisations, multinational corporations and individuals.
Core Beliefs	States are self-interested actors.	States are cooperative and work in abidance with international norms and international law.
Security	Security can best be achieved by maximising military power.	Security can best be achieved by cooperation, mutual gain and abiding to moral/ethical/legal principles.

5.2.8 Debrief

A list of questions for students to reflect on what they have learnt from the game and for facilitators to understand how effective the game was/what gaps occurred. This can also include take-home questions for students to continue reflecting and learning on the skills that were covered in the session.

> *Do you think one of the two theories chosen provides a realistic assessment of a state's international response to a pandemic outbreak?*
>
> *Which actors do you think you need to involve for effective crisis management at the national level?*
>
> *Which international approach (Realism or Idealism) would be more effective in dealing with a pandemic?*
>
> *Reflecting on past and present pandemics (e.g., COVID-19), can you provide examples of states that followed a Realist perspective in their international response to a pandemic?*
>
> *How did the scenario make you feel?*
>
> *Optional: To integrate students further into the development of this game and to improve the experience for future students, students could be asked to write feedback on Post-it notes and place these on a whiteboard/wall where the educator creates two different sections: (1) "What did I like about this session". (2) "Room for improvement".*

5.2.9 Handouts and Material

The following guide is not a necessity for the simulation game. In some iterations where I used this guide, it aided students in structuring and clarifying their thoughts. At times, however, I observed the negative effect of some groups following this structure too rigorously, thus undermining the free flow

Copyright material from Hirani & Varin 2003, *Supporting Adult Learners through Games and Interactive Teaching*, Routledge

Table 5.2 Possible Student Guide

	RESPONSE/ACTIONS TAKEN
DOMESTIC	
Social	
Economic	
Military	
INTERNATIONAL	

of the simulation and students becoming less effective in their response articulation (Table 5.2).

5.3 Adaptation of the Games to a Different Context

Climate change has caused a resource crisis, and states struggle to obtain the necessary resources (water, food, energy) for maintaining the security and prosperity of their populations. Students are divided into four groups. Students are asked to develop a state response to this crisis. This response needs to identify internal and international measures to be taken. Each group is assigned an IR theory (e.g., Realism, Idealism), which will guide their international response. The educator will choose a specific state that students will use to develop their responses.

- *Scenario*

Climate change has led to an unprecedented resource crisis (water, food, energy). You are in charge of drafting a state's response to this crisis, taking both domestic and international responses into account.

- *Scenario objectives*

Identify domestic vulnerabilities and international objectives/interests. Establish responses across three domestic trajectories (social, economic, military) based

Copyright material from Hirani & Varin 2003, *Supporting Adult Learners through Games and Interactive Teaching*, Routledge

on the vulnerabilities identified. Establish an international response based on the international objectives/interests set and the IR theory given.

Bibliography

Blanton, R. G. (2021). Zombies and international relations: a simple guide for bringing the undead into your classroom. *International Studies Perspectives*, 14(1), pp. 1–13.

Burke, L. A. and Moore, J. E. (2003). A perennial dilemma in OB education: Engaging the traditional student. *Academy of Management Learning & Education*, 2(37), p. 52.

Clark, D. B., Sengupta, P., Brady, C. E., Martinez-Garza, M. M., and Killingsworth, S. S. (2015). Disciplinary integration of digital games for science learning. *International Journal of STEM Education*, 2(1), pp. 1–21.

Doyle, D. and Brown, W. F. (2000). Using a business simulation to teach applied skills—the benefits and challenges of using student teams from multiple counties. *Journal of European Industrial Training*, 24, pp. 330–6.

Drezner, D. W. (2011). *Theories of international politics and zombies*. Princeton, New Jersey: Princeton University Press.

Gaydos, M. J. and Devane, B. M. (2019). Designing for identity in game-based learning. *Mind, Culture, and Activity*, 26(1), pp. 61–74.

Horn, L., Rubin, O. and Schouenborg, L. (2016). Undead pedagogy: How a zombie simulation can contribute to teaching IR. *International Studies Perspectives*, 17(2), pp. 187–201.

Kreber, C. (2001). Learning experientially through case studies? A conceptual analysis. *Teaching in Higher Education*, 6(2), pp. 217–28.

McCarthy, M. M. (2014). The role of games and simulations to teach abstract concepts of anarchy, cooperation, and conflict in world politics. *Journal of Political Science Education*, 10(4), pp. 400–13.

McClintock, C. (2000). Creating communities of practice for experiential learning in policy studies. In: Ralston P.A., Lerner, R. M., Mullis, A. K., Simerly, C. B. and Murray, J. B., eds., *Social change, public policy, and community collaborations*. Boston: Springer, pp. 33–51.

Reid, M., Brown, S. and Tabibzadeh, K. (2012). Capstone teaching models: Combining simulation, analytical intuitive learning processes, history and effectiveness. *Journal of Education for Business*, 87(3), pp. 178–84.

Salminen-Tuomaala, Mari and Koskela, Tiina (2020). How can simulation help with learning project work skills? *Experiences from Higher Education in Finland, Educational Research*, 62(1), pp. 77–94.

Shaffer, D. W. (2006). Epistemic frames for epistemic games. *Computers & Education*, 46(3), pp. 223–34.

Shellman, Stephen M. and Turan, Kürşad (2006). Do simulations enhance student learning? An empirical evaluation of an IR simulation. *Journal of Political Science Education*, 2(1), pp. 19–32.

Wolf, J. and Luethge, D. J. (2003). The impact of involvement on performance in business simulations: An examination of Goosen's "know little" decision-making thesis. *Journal of Education for Business*, 79(2), pp. 69–74.

6 Playful Mocktails Competition©
Developing Empathy

Ed Gonsalves

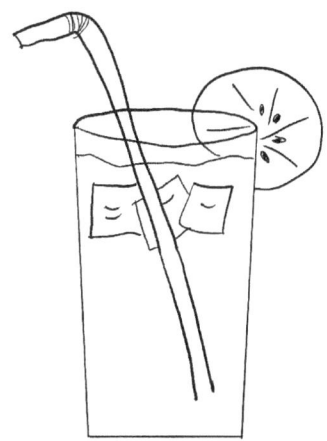

6.1 Overview

This chapter cements our understanding of how experiential learning can be enhanced and developed in business workshops using playfulness as a design value (Bakker et al. 2020). It describes the author's design, development and delivery of modular workshop activities to create opportunities for playful learning when expanding participants' entrepreneurial and empathic capacities.

The workshop is designed using an activity-based learning approach (Engeström 2001) and participatory methods (Massa & O'Mahony 2021) in which all participants are co-learners in a collaborative, peer-learning, open environment. It is based on Engeström's expansive learning triangle (Figure 6.1) in which artefacts, activities and relationships are designed to change the perspectives and practices of participants from egocentric to eco-centric dialogues.

It offers insights and resources into how ethical, entrepreneurial, and empathic education can be delivered in innovative and effective ways that mirror the 'real-world' experience of existing founders and advocates of the Lean Start-Up philosophies (Blank 2013). It also offers insights into the

DOI: 10.4324/9781003230120-6

48 Ed Gonsalves

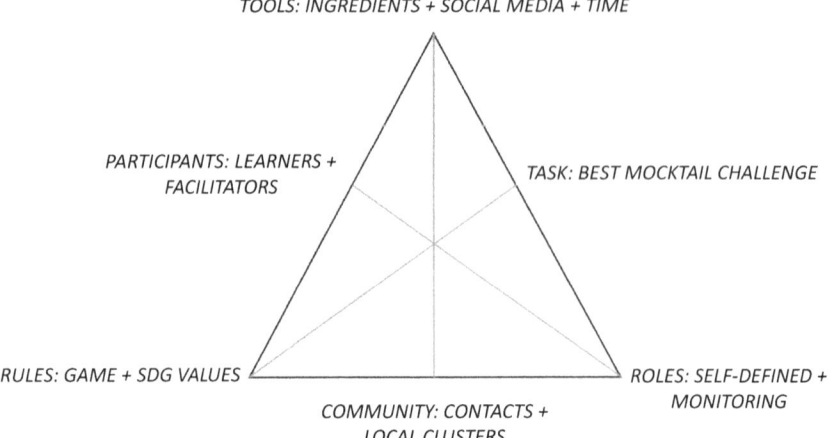

Figure 6.1 Engeström's expansive learning triangle for playful mocktail competition©.

nature and use of playfulness within entrepreneurial workshops that extend beyond educational settings – e.g., organisational, managerial and culturally embedded settings.

Expansive learning involves participants gaining an awareness of their current habits of the mind and resulting points of view. These are accompanied by a transparent critique of participant and community assumptions, premises, an assessment of alternative views, a decision to negate an old perspective or view in favour of a new one, or to make a synthesis of old and new, resulting in more justified beliefs to guide action. The workshops can also be used to demonstrate how a transformation in teaching perspective can be achieved through activity-based learning models that involve inquiry and interactive teaching. However, implementing the workshop for transformation of professional teaching practices will require additional sustained support. The workshop does offer a viable means of exploring transformative learning in entrepreneurial settings (Figure 6.1).

We know customers don't buy products; they buy solutions to problems – and customers' problems are best described by the customers. Despite this, most founders spend forever developing solutions and very little time examining whether customers want these. This game will show your participants an engaging and experiential way to identify and be inspired by customers' real-world problems in a particularly fun and easily accessible product space.

Participants in this game construct knowledge; they don't receive it. They learn by doing and failing. This failure drives them to ask questions and seek answers through active exploration by interaction with customers. Participants competing as teams fail quickly, and instructors can help them regroup, process and take aim again. It is iterative and interactive and hones the fundamental skill of deep and active listening: a foundation for building customer empathy and a customer empathy map.

The deep listening skills and development of empathy are pertinent in many contexts within which the 'other' is paramount to the success of an initiative/project/investment raise. For example, we have also used the game in user experience and design contexts. Facilitators can also reconfigure the game so that the emphasis is on inter-team cooperation and collaboration rather than purely about customer centricity. The game can be flipped to focus on resource planning and negotiation in supplier-side contexts.

You can try these exercises and share feedback on how they worked for you. Share your experience with this exercise and how you adapt it; get your participants learning by doing. You can tag those experiences with us on the game's Instagram feed: https://www.instagram.com/mocktailweek/.

We suggest that the feedback from previous participants will provide facilitators and instructors with ideas for adapting this game into alternative contexts. Previous participants have reported that this exercise has challenged them to apply theory and to develop practice. Some examples of ideas generated in this exercise have included the following:

1. *Finance:* How to frame pitching to Business Angel Incubators as a sales and negotiation process, where business angels compete over new venture ideas.
2. *Culture:* The exercise provided participants with the need to be open-minded and accept divergent as well as convergent values that have a positive impact on venturing – e.g., discussions about the values implied in alcoholic versus non-alcoholic innovation and advertising, debating healthy diets and ingredients across variable cultures and value systems. How does the link with United Nations Sustainable Development Goals (UN-SDG) raise ethical concerns around business methods, ingredient supplies, promotion and pricing?
3. *Network Effects:* The survival of ideas may be driven by whether the start-up can assemble and leverage a team, and how well the team networks in the target market. Development of peer-to-peer networks and experienced agents (e.g., senior mentors) to mobilise business networks for new and nascent challenges in participants' personal lives. There is a need to consider the extent to which participants are always operating in larger ecosystems of networks, well-wishers and supporters to which they can turn to for crowd resourcing in all kinds of projects and other fields as well.
4. *Motivating Ownership of New Challenges:* Engage and incentivise workshop members to build product review networks to provide feedback on new products/markets. In sum, participants often stated how the exercise challenged them to connect the unconnected in a contrarian manner and to identify high-impact recommendations to support entrepreneurship among multiple stakeholders.

"The Customer Is King" paradigm is deeply ingrained in the way we teach, execute and think about enterprise. And as omnipresent as consumer psychology methods are in our day-to-day, they hold geometrically larger real estate in our subconscious models about what a business is and how we relate to it.

The instructor's skills-challenges offered here require highly energetic, deliberate and disruptive efforts on the part of educators. To graduate entrepreneurs with a 21st-century skill set, the instructor must both lower the barrier to applying these new techniques through practice and fundamentally change the way learners think about new ventures to motivate their use. The exercises challenge educators to evolve from the case method improvement on pure theory and participate in today's cutting-edge experiential learning practices to deliver key skills for today's entrepreneurs. The activities' pedagogic goal is to build up critical gravity for the use of experiential learning in applied entrepreneurship. We hope fellow educators will consider trying these techniques in the classroom and share how they work for them and their learning and frustrations on how to help today's entrepreneurs create better ventures using playful activity-based, everyday materials as objects for transformative learning.

6.2 Games Details

6.2.1 Key Skills

Customer empathy, 'peer and customer listening', active creativity, negotiating, bootstrapping, effectual thinking, design by bricolage thinking, learning from failure, solution iteration

6.2.2 Group Size

- This game can be played with 9–60 people.
- It is a team competition.
- A team consists of three (min) to six (max) players.
- A minimum of three teams compete.

6.2.3 Time

Plan for approximately 45–120 minutes for this game: depending on the size and number of participating teams, and the medium for delivery: offline versus online.

6.2.4 Purpose (Learning Objectives)

1. To develop an understanding of the need to experiment with assumptions about customers when building products in a start-up
2. To 'get-out-of-the-building' and learn to be 'punched in the face' by the market. To fail and succeed
3. To break the paradigm of "a market of one customer: myself"

4. To fail and iterate fast
5. To experientially learn the entrepreneurial principle of bird-in-the-hand

6.2.5 Preparation and Setup

- Room –
  - This exercise can be instructed/facilitated either on or offline. In both instances, facilitators are advised to use a whiteboard, flipchart or stickies to capture rules, hygiene instructions, learnings, seed questions and scoreboards. If offline, observation of the process and dynamic in large conferences or classrooms is fairly straightforward.
- The activity may be conducted with no materials or setup; the use of stickies or notecards, a flipchart, chalkboard or audio visual setup are, however, recommended. Stickies or note cards offer a record of the full set of innovations which may be of separate value. Instructors should distribute one sticky note or note card to each participant and ensure that writing instruments are available. Similarly, instructors may prefer a learning space that facilitates ease of participants' movement, though key lessons may be gained in spaces that restrict learners' mobility. Backgrounds on drivers of innovation may be provided at the instructor's discretion and in line with pedagogical preferences.
- Specific, supplementary resources for facilitators and instructors are provided at the end of the game setup details section.
- Tech –
  a. All the above can be simulated using online whiteboards, such as Miro board, in conjunction with virtual meeting facilities – e.g., Zoom.

(Additional Resources)

- Ingredient suggestions and allocations that each participant needs to secure prior to the exercise can be found in Annex A or at this link: https://bit.ly/2CzI0Kh. The list is a suggestion and the facilitators can either secure the items on the list themselves in advance, or they can develop a new list for students using ingredients that can be locally and cheaply found.
- An example of how this exercise can be gamified can be found in Annex B or at this link: https://bit.ly/31X7YzW. You can copy and customise it for your purposes. We suggest that you do not reveal the performance criteria to participants in advance. Having run the activity once, you can use a leaderboard or scoreboard to motivate the participants to play a second round of the exercise. In the second round, you may reveal the scores to the participants alongside the performance criteria. We also suggest that you only reveal the leaderboard or scoreboard after your first learning debrief and not before.

6.2.6 Instructions

Build Customer Empathy through Assumption Testing: Validate or Falsify Pains, Gains and Discover Your Evangelists

Challenge: A client is about to launch his new mocktail bar in Barcelona. He has asked you to help. He wants to take full advantage of market trends and have an impact on UN-SDG goals. He likes you and wants you and your team to demonstrate your capabilities in this area!

Your Mission:

"To make the world's most "Instagrammable mocktail" to launch Barcelona mocktail week 202x (x represents the current year) and put his new bar on the map".

To take part, each team has to contribute one clock policewoman/man.

The client has given us access to what they see as one of their key resources: their new Instagram (mocktailweek) and Twitter Feeds (@MocktailWeek).
You Have Ten Minutes to Complete Your Customer Profile Map

1. Every minute over time costs you 10% in the eye of the client
2. Demographic, where they live (postcode), where they work and play, where they consume, where you will access/find them easily and relaxed
3. Gain, pains, jobs

You Have 3 Minutes to Prepare for Delivery of the Customer Profile Map – every minute over time costs you 10% in the eye of the client

You Have 15 Minutes to Deliver the Customer Profile Map – every minute over time costs you 10% in the eye of the client

Reflection: What did you do?

1. Research
2. Team wastage
3. Resource duplication
4. Beyond the room

Reflection: What assumptions did you make about the following?

1. Your customer
2. What they want: package, place, moment
3. Taste

Reflection: What did you learn?

1. What do you need to discover about your customer?
2. How can you do that in 5 minutes and better understand them qualitatively and quantitatively?

You Have a Break:

1. Twenty minutes to complete the survey: https://forms.gle/YPE4jKDhNnzHtazn7 or create your own
2. Re-launch to discover and clear the room
3. Every 30 seconds over time costs you 10% in the eye of the client

Time to Experiment and Learn from Your 'Evangelists'

1. Problem: at the very beginning of your start-up path, you'll need to test whether an issue you identified is considered important by your target audience.
2. Experimentation is used to discover: to empathise with your customer.
3. Experimentation is used primarily to learn faster by testing with real customers in order to understand how they will engage with your business idea. It is, therefore, crucial to define the goal of what you are trying to learn before launching an experiment.

6.2.7 Guidance

The instructor may remind participants:

The best ideas are not guaranteed market success.

The role of the entrepreneurial team is critical to market success, often generating unexpected or entirely unpredictable outcomes.

The entrepreneur team does not have to be the same persons as the idea team: they can form alliances and oust members.

Some drivers of market success may be partly or entirely out of the team's or entrepreneur's control.

Great ideas and innovations are drivers of UN-SDG change.

Instructors are encouraged to make the full set of ideas available to participants after the activity for their own edification.

6.2.8 Debrief

The following is a list of initial questions for learners to reflect on what they have learnt from the challenge and for facilitators to understand how effective the challenge was and what learning gaps appeared. This can also include takeaway questions for participants to reflect on after the workshop, for homework, for example. You can also ask them to complete this Learning Form Template: https://forms.gle/WZXCcDw9jNwWEeHL9.

What did you do?
What did you research?
What time wastage did you experience?
What resource duplication did you observe?
Did you move beyond the room?
What assumptions did you make about your customer?
What assumptions did you make about what they want: package, place, price, moment, taste?
What did you learn?
What about the exercise surprised you the most?
What do you think went wrong with your initial plan?

What did you learn by interacting with your customers that you couldn't have predicted in your business plan?

What do you need to discover about your customer?

How can you do that in 5 minutes and better understand them qualitatively and quantitatively?

Samples of the types of previous responses that the facilitators/instructors can reference can be found here: https://bit.ly/2Y9NIKn.

6.3 Adaptation of the Games to a Different Context

This exercise can be changed around to suit multiple contexts with a variety of skill developments in mind. The playful and fun nature of the sequencing of activities allows you, as the facilitator/instructor, to re-order sequences, materials or learning intentions to suit your specific contextual setting, be they intra- or inter-organisational settings.

For example, the activity could be used to develop team-building skill sets and developing team leadership competences:

First of all – use your imagination – you can simplify, adapt, shorten and lengthen most of the sub-activities presented in this exercise. To turn this gamified version into a quick activity or warm-up, scale down the materials, shorten the time allowed and make the exercise easier. Most of the sub-activities can also be used for participants' personal and not necessarily curricula-driven education and development, and for induction or exit stages of a team-based course – adapt them to suit. The number of members per team affects activity time and complexity – teams of four or more need a leader and tend to take longer than a pair or team of three. Increasing or reducing team size and introducing or removing the team-leader requirement are simple ideas for increasing or reducing game complexity and exercise duration. Allow teams to negotiate mergers and alliances by stretching the exercise over more than one session.

Annex A

Table A.1 Resource List for Allocation to Students to Bring

Resourcer Name	Item	Quantity
Students 1 and 2	**Large fresh mint leaves**	1 bunch
Students 3 and 4	**Limes**	3
Students 5 and 6	**Bottle of Sprite**	1/2L
Students 7 and 8	**Orange juice**	1L
Students 9 and 10	**Bottle of tonic water**	1/2L
Students 11 and 12	**Bottle of ginger beer**	1/2L
Students 13 and 14	**Pomegranate juice**	1L

(Continued)

Table A.1 (Continued) Resource List for Allocation to Students to Bring

Resourcer Name	Item	Quantity
Students 15 and 16	**Strawberries**	6
Students 17 and 18	**Raspberries**	12
Students 19 and 20	**Pineapple**	1
Students 21 and 22	**Clear honey**	1
Students 23 and 24	**Blackcurrant cordial**	1
Students 25 and 26	**Coconut water**	1L
Students 27 and 28	**Caster sugar**	small packet
Students 29 and 30	**Brown sugar**	small packet
Students 31 and 32	**Lemons**	6

Annex B

Table B.1 Crowd Mocktail Scoreboard

This scoreboard should be used to assess every team. The crowd will jointly determine the scores for each criterion.

Appearance and Interaction (maximum score of 10 for each criterion)

Criteria	Crowd Score
Neatness	
Interaction with crowd	
Originality	
Showmanship	
Cleanliness	

Difficulty and Presentation (maximum score of 10 for each criterion)

Criteria	Crowd Score
Variety of images	
Ease of recipe	
Combination with music	
Originality – creativity	

Execution (maximum score of 10 for each criterion)

Criteria	Crowd Score
Colour	
Smoothness	
Control	
Pours	
Confidence	

Deductions (maximum −1 for each criterion)

Criteria	Deduction
Drops	
Fumbles	
Spills	

Table B.2 Tutor Mocktail Scoreboard (Maximum Ten for Each Criterion)

This scoreboard should be used to assess every team. A score should only be provided if the team was the first to meet the criteria before all other teams.

Criteria	Score
First to ask non-team members inside room what they would like	
First to ask non-team members outside room what they would like	
First to mix and test with others in their team	
First to mix and test with others not in their team	
First to mix and test with others not in the room	
First to walk around and see other teams' ingredients	
First to offer to exchange ingredients with other teams	
First to offer two teams to work together in a joint venture	
First to fail	
Second to fail	
First to iterate once	
First to iterate twice	
First to price mocktail	
First to secure an order	
First to use social media to test and capture reactions	
First to iterate from social media feedback	
Highest positive feedback from first iteration of social media	
Highest positive feedback from second iteration of social media	

Deductions (maximum −10 for each criterion)

Criteria	Deduction
No iteration	
No testing in the room	
No testing out of the room	
No customer taste notes	
No customer question notes	
No iteration from external customers	
No iteration from in the room customers	
No inter-team collaboration	
No ingredient exchange	
No social media tests	
Time: 1 point for every 5 seconds over time	

Bibliography

Bakker, A., Scharp, Y., Breevaart, K., & De Vries, J. (2020). Playful work design: introduction of a new concept. *The Spanish Journal of Psychology*, *23*. https://doi.org/10.1017/SJP.2020.20

Blank, S. (2013, May 1). Why the lean start-up changes everything. *Harvard Business Review*. https://hbr.org/2013/05/why-the-lean-start-up-changes-everything

Engeström, Y. (2001). Expansive learning at work: toward an activity theoretical reconceptualization. *Journal of Education and Work*, *14*(1), pp. 133–56. https://doi.org/10.1080/13639080020028747

Massa, F. G., & O'Mahony, S. (2021). Order from chaos: how networked activists self-organize by creating a participation architecture. *Administrative Science Quarterly*, 00018392211008880. https://doi.org/10.1177/00018392211008880

7 Developing a Strategy to Play Monopoly™ Using Mathematical Techniques and Explore Various Analytical Methods

Sahil Shah

7.1 Overview

Developing a robot, pseudo-algorithm or pre-meditated strategy to play Monopoly™ in order to learn and explore application of statistical probability, economic inflation and strategy in decision-making. The desired transferable skill sets are for students to learn the following:

- Basic mathematical techniques (which are sometimes taught in school without context) can be applied to practical situations
- To present mathematical models using data visualisation techniques in order to easily persuade less technical audiences on how tactical decisions in the game are best made

These skill sets are in heavy demand across technology and data-driven organisations, especially during the current technology revolution.

Monopoly is a turn-based board game where players assume the role of property traders and developers. The game requires players to make a multitude of decisions throughout the game, but there is also a stochastic element

DOI: 10.4324/9781003230120-7

introduced into the game by the roll of dice. The randomness of the dice often creates the perception that the outcome is based on luck but lesser known to many people there are certain strategies that can be employed to enhance your fortunes in the game.

This chapter outlines distinct topics for discussion which can all be explored individually in isolation or combined together to challenge students in applying an analytical approach to the game and derive ways of developing a winning strategy.

7.2 Games Details

7.2.1 Key Skills

Strategy development, data analysis, data visualisation, critical thinking

7.2.2 Group Size

Any group from two to six people. Students might learn best when placed in pairs to discuss ideas first and then gather the larger group to compile learnings.

7.2.3 Time

One-hour sessions should adequately allow room for discussion in pairs followed by larger group exercises.

7.2.4 Purpose (Learning Objectives)

1. How to define effective and relevant performance metrics for assessing player success
2. How to determine the probability of a player landing on a specific place on the board given a specific starting configuration
3. How to assess different board property parameters and understand their effectiveness in achieving the Key Performance Indicators set in item 1
4. How to develop a strategy to play the game when faced with decision-making situations

7.2.5 Preparation and Setup

Each session would need a visual representation of the board visible at all times, which can be found in Appendix A. This can be printed out if a board is not readily available. Along with the board, other sessions might benefit from having visibility of the other props in the game:

Property title deeds (these are listed in a matrix in Appendix A)
2 x six-sided dice

16 x Chance cards (or at least show the description on each card)
16 x Community Chest cards (or at least show the description on each card)

Alternatively, students can be provided with printouts of Appendices A, B, C and D, which show the layout of the board (Appendix A), content of Chance cards (Appendix B), Community Chest (Appendix C) cards and the prices for properties (Appendix D).

7.2.6 Guidance

Students who are unfamiliar with the game would probably benefit from playing it during their first session to appreciate the decision-making that players need to make.

7.2.7 Instructions

7.2.7.1 Part 1

The Classic Monopoly Rules can be found in the Endnotes at the URL,[1] which is published and hosted by the game's manufacturer. There are now multiple versions of the Monopoly board, and they vary between different markets. A UK-centric version of the board can be found in Appendix A, which also contains a linear layout of the board which is sometimes easier to understand when assessing the board for academic purposes.

7.2.7.2 Part 2

In this section, questions are grouped based on the following three themes:

Defining Performance Metrics
Probabilities and Dice Mechanics
Property Trading

The facilitator should pause the gameplay at various stages of the game to ask the questions relating to each theme. Ideally, the questions should be asked at the beginning, halfway through the game and at the end of the game. This will enable the players to improve their knowledge and answering as they progress through the gameplay.

7.2.7.2.1 DEFINING PERFORMANCE METRICS

7.2.7.2.1.1 Methods of Increasing Wealth During the game, players increase their wealth via several methods of which not all are immediately obvious (Table 7.1).

Table 7.1 Wealth Method Questions

Question No	Question
1	What are the different methods of increasing a player's wealth in the game?
2	For each method identified, consider whether it is driven by random events or by player-initiated actions.

Table 7.2 Wealth Method Answers

Method	Description	Shorthand	Initiated By
1	Passing the "Go" space and collecting GBP 200 each time.	Passing "Go"	Random event
2	Collecting rent from other players landing on properties you have invested in.	Rent	Combination of random events and player-initiated action
3	Collecting income from random events in the Chance and Community Chest cards.	Chance/Community Chest	Random event
4	Agreeing to sell a title deed or Chance/Community Chest card to a fellow player.	Trading	Player-initiated

Students can be prompted if needed to collectively be able to come up with the methods listed in Table 7.2.

For a further more complex understanding of methods of increasing wealth, refer to Appendix 1.

7.2.7.2.1.2 Wealth Asset Types Assets players can collect during the game extend beyond cash. Listing these can also be a class exercise if the facilitator sees value in ensuring students understand the game mechanics (Table 7.3).

Table 7.3 Wealth Asset Type Questions

Question No	Question
1	What are the different forms of wealth or asset types a player can accumulate?
2	For assets other than cash, how do you estimate the total value of the asset in monetary terms?
3	For non-cash assets, should the monetary value be based on historic acquisition cost or future earning potential?
4	Which assets further enhance the primary objective of bankrupting other players based on the methods of increasing wealth?

Table 7.4 Wealth Asset Type Answers

Asset Type	How to Quantify in Monetary Terms
Cash	Cash value
Property title deeds	Expected rental receipts based on N number of players' turns
Houses and hotels developed on title deeds	Expected rental receipts based on N number of players' turns
"Get out of jail free" cards	Cash payment avoided when used to escape jail

Students can be prompted if needed to collectively be able to come up with the methods listed in Table 7.4.

For a complex explanation of challenging metric selection, refer to Appendix 2.

7.2.7.2.2 PROBABILITIES AND DICE MECHANICS

Moving through the Monopoly board is governed primarily by rolling two 6-sided dice. Often this fools players into thinking that landing on particular spaces is entirely random.

However, there are two factors which could be explored to challenge the assumption of randomness (see Tables 7.5 and 7.6).

Table 7.5 Single Dice Roll Questions

Question No	Question
1	If two 6-sided dice are rolled each turn, what are all the possible outcomes?
2	For each outcome, what is the probability of that outcome occurring?

Table 7.6 Possibility Space to Map Dice Roll Outcomes Based on Inputs from Two 6-Sided Dice

		Die 1					
		1	2	3	4	5	6
Die 2	1	2	3	4	5	6	7
	2	3	4	5	6	7	8
	3	4	5	6	7	8	9
	4	5	6	7	8	9	10
	5	6	7	8	9	10	11
	6	7	8	9	10	11	12

Table 7.7 Frequency of Possible Dice Roll Outcomes from Single Roll of Two Dice

Outcome	Frequency	Probability (%)	Fractional Probability
2	1	2.8%	1/36
3	2	5.6%	2/36
4	3	8.3%	3/36
5	4	11.1%	4/36
6	5	13.9%	5/36
7	6	16.7%	6/36
8	5	13.9%	5/36
9	4	11.1%	4/36
10	3	8.3%	3/36
11	2	5.6%	2/36
12	1	2.8%	1/36

7.2.7.2.2.1 Single Roll Dice Probability Distribution Students should be asked to draw up Tables 7.6 and 7.7 where the grey boxes are the answers students should fill out. Through discussion, they can gradually build up the frequency distribution graph in Figure 7.1 to understand that moving through the board is not entirely random, but rather pseudo-random.

For a more complex explanation of Multiple Roll Dice Probability Distribution, refer to Appendix 3.

7.2.7.2.2.2 Other Board-Driven Player Moves Moving through the board is sometimes also governed by factors other than an individual dice roll (Table 7.8).

Students can be prompted if needed to collectively be able to come up with the methods listed in Table 7.9.

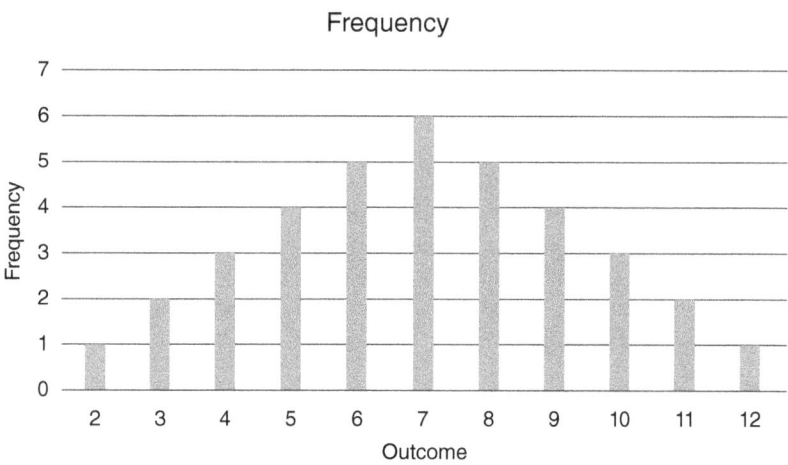

Figure 7.1 Frequency distribution visualisation.

Table 7.8 Board-Driven Player Moves Questions

Question No	Question
1	Other than rolling doubles three times consecutively, what other methods are there for a player to land in jail?
2	What is the probability of those other methods occurring?

Table 7.9 Board-Driven Player Move Answers

Factor Type	Explanation
Landing on "Go to jail" square	The "Go to jail" (square number 31) space dictates that any player immediately goes to jail regardless of their dice roll.
Rolling three doubles in a row	Players who roll three 'doubles' in a row are immediately sent to jail regardless of where they are on the board.
Chance and Community Chest cards	Chance and Community Chest cards (as described in Appendix B and Appendix C, respectively) sometimes dictate that players move to different spaces on the board. In each set of 16 cards, one card sends the player to jail.
Global board probability distribution	Based on the combination of factors explored in probability and dice mechanics, students should explore the global board probability distribution (frequency of players landing on any of the 40 board spaces in steady state – i.e., long after the first few dice rolls are completed and any transient probability biases associated with starting on the "Go" space are diluted).

Table 7.10 Uniform Probability Questions

Question No	Question
1	Is it right to assume that each space on the board has an equal chance of being landed on?
2	Assuming player position on the board is unknown, is the probability of landing on any given space equal to 1/40?"

7.2.7.2.2.3 Uniform Probability Distribution Based on the factor types described, students should start to realise that the number of entry routes into the jail space (square number 11) are greater than the number of entry routes into other spaces on the board Table 7.10.

For a more complex explanation of computing probability distribution, refer to Appendix 4.

7.2.7.2.3 PROPERTY TRADING

Players collect property title deeds throughout the game to increase their earning power. In general, a single-coloured set of properties is worth more

Developing a Strategy to Play Monopoly™ 65

Table 7.11 Property Trading Questions

Question No	Question
1	When constructing a decision-making algorithm to govern how a robot player would purchase properties, how would you devise a decision-making process to govern purchasing from the bank and from other players?

collectively compared with the sum of its individual parts due to the ability to collect:

Double rent when left undeveloped, or
Enhanced rent when developed with houses/hotels.

Properties may be acquired by purchasing them from the bank (when not already owned by other players) or by offering to purchase them from other players (Table 7.11).

Since properties may only be purchased from the bank when a player lands on the corresponding board space, the decision-making algorithm only needs to be invoked when that condition is fulfilled.

A simple algorithm may follow the flow of Figure 7.2.

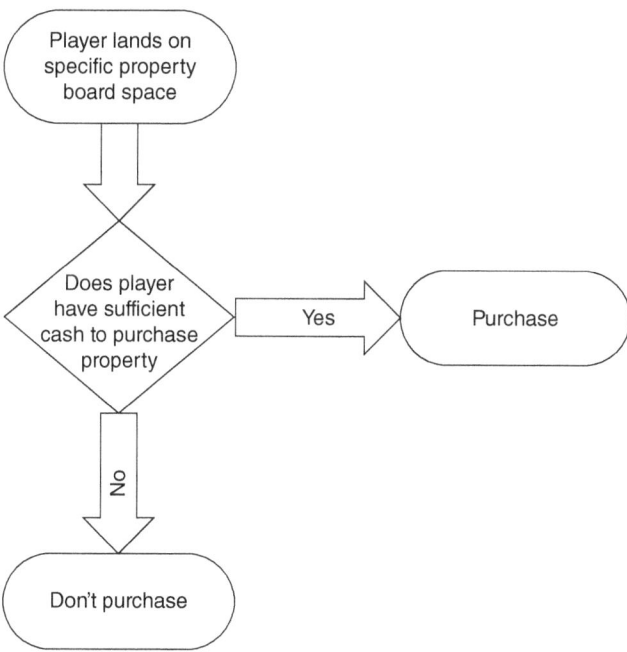

Figure 7.2 Property trading flow diagram.

For a complex explanation of purchasing from the bank, refer to Appendix 5. For a complex version of purchasing from other players refer to Appendix 6.

7.2.8 Debrief

Gather in plenary once the game has been played for 1 hour and all three question themes from Part 2 under the instructions have been answered. Ask participants to reflect on the following questions:

What did you learn about defining performance metrics?
What did you learn about probabilities and dice mechanics?
What did you learn about property trading?
If you were to play this game again, what would you do differently and why?
What have you learnt about decision-making and strategic thinking from this exercise?

Appendix A

Table A.1 Title Deeds

Square Number	Square Name	Square Type	Property Group Identity*	Book Cost (GBP)
1	Go	Stationary Space		
2	Old Kent Road	Scalable Property	A	60
3	Community Chest	Action Space		
4	Whitechapel Road	Scalable Property	A	60
5	Income Tax	Action Space		
6	Kings Cross Station	Non-scalable Property	X	200
7	The Angel Islington	Scalable Property	B	100
8	Chance	Action Space		
9	Euston Road	Scalable Property	B	100
10	Pentonville Road	Scalable Property	B	120
11	Jail	Stationary Space		
12	Pall Mall	Scalable Property	C	140
13	Electric Company	Non-scalable Property	Y	150
14	Whitehall	Scalable Property	C	140
15	Northumberland Avenue	Scalable Property	C	160

(*Continued*)

Table A.1 (Continued) Title Deeds

Square Number	Square Name	Square Type	Property Group Identity*	Book Cost (GBP)
16	Marylebone Station	Non-scalable Property	X	200
17	Bow Street	Scalable Property	D	180
18	Community Chest	Action Space		
19	Marlborough Street	Scalable Property	D	180
20	Vine Street	Scalable Property	D	200
21	Free Parking	Stationary Space		
22	Strand	Scalable Property	E	220
23	Chance	Action Space		
24	Fleet Street	Scalable Property	E	220
25	Trafalgar Square	Scalable Property	E	240
26	Fenchurch Street	Non-scalable Property	X	200
27	Leicester Square	Scalable Property	F	260
28	Coventry Street	Scalable Property	F	260
29	Water Works	Non-scalable Property	Y	150
30	Piccadilly	Scalable Property	F	280
31	Go To Jail	Action Space		
32	Regent Street	Scalable Property	G	300
33	Oxford Street	Scalable Property	G	300
34	Community Chest	Action Space		
35	Bond Street	Scalable Property	G	320
36	Liverpool St. Station	Non-scalable Property	X	200
37	Chance	Action Space		
38	Park Lane	Scalable Property	H	350
39	Super Tax	Action Space		
40	Mayfair	Scalable Property	H	400

* Spaces which represent properties where the title deed can be acquired are labelled with a letter denoting which group of properties the title deed belongs to.

Table A.2 Board Layout

	1	2	3	4	5	6	7	8	9	10	
	Go	Old Kent Road	Community Chest	Whitechapel Road	Income Tax	Kings Cross Station	The Angel Islington	Chance	Euston Road	Pentonville Road	Jail
40	Mayfair											11
39	Super Tax											12	Pall Mall
												13	Electric Company
38	Park Lane											14	Whitehall
37	Chance											15	Northumberland Avenue
36	Liverpool St. Station											16	Marylebone Station
35	Bond Street											17	Bow Street
34	Community Chest											18	Community Chest
33	Oxford Street											19	Marlborough Street
32	Regent Street											20	Vine Street
31	Go to Jail	30	29	28	27	26	25	24	23	22	21
		Piccadilly	Water Works	Coventry Street	Leicester Square	Fenchurch Street	Trafalgar Square	Fleet Street	Chance	Strand	Free Parking

Appendix B

Table B.1 Chance Cards Content

Card ID	Card Content
1	Advance to Go (Collect £200)
2	Advance to Trafalgar Square. If you pass Go, collect £200
3	Advance to Mayfair
4	Advance to Pall Mall. If you pass Go, collect £200
5	Advance to the nearest Station. If unowned, you may buy it from the Bank. If owned, pay owner twice the rental to which they are otherwise entitled
6	Advance to the nearest Station. If unowned, you may buy it from the Bank. If owned, pay owner twice the rental to which they are otherwise entitled
7	Advance token to nearest Utility. If unowned, you may buy it from the Bank. If owned, throw dice and pay the owner a total ten times the amount thrown
8	Bank pays you dividend of £50
9	Get Out of Jail Free. This card may be kept until needed or traded/sold
10	Go back three spaces
11	Go to Jail. Go directly to Jail, do not pass Go, do not collect £200
12	Make general repairs on all your property. For each house pay £25. For each hotel pay £100
13	Speeding fine £15
14	Take a trip to Kings Cross Station. If you pass Go, collect £200
15	You have been elected Chairman of the Board. Pay each player £50
16	Your building loan matures. Collect £150

Appendix C

Table C.1 Community Chest Cards Content

Card ID	Card Content
1	Advance to Go (Collect £200)
2	Bank error in your favour. Collect £200
3	Doctor's fee. Pay £50
4	From sale of stock, you get £50
5	Get out of jail free
6	Go to Jail. Go directly to jail, do not pass Go, do not collect £200
7	Holiday fund matures. Receive £100
8	Income tax refund. Collect £20
9	It is your birthday. Collect £10 from every player
10	Life insurance matures. Collect £100

(*Continued*)

Table C.1 (Continued)

Card ID	Card Content
11	Pay hospital fees of £100
12	Pay school fees of £50
13	Receive £25 consultancy fee
14	You are assessed for street repairs. £40 per house. £115 per hotel
15	You have won second prize in a beauty contest. Collect £10
16	You inherit £100

Appendix D

Table D.1 Prices for Properties

Square Name	Book Cost	Development Cost	Rent					
			Number of Houses					
			0	1	2	3	4	Hotel
Go								
Old Kent Road	60	50	2	10				
Community Chest								
Whitechapel Road	60	50	4	20				
Income Tax								
Kings Cross Station*	200			25	50	100	200	
The Angel Islington	100	50	6	30	90	270	400	550
Chance								
Euston Road	100	50	6	30	90	270	400	550
Pentonville Road	120	50	8	40	100	300	450	600
Jail								
Pall Mall	140	100	10	50	150	450	625	750
Electric Company**	150			4 x dice	10 x dice			
Whitehall	140	100	10	50	150	450	625	750
Northumberland Avenue	160	100	12	60	180	500	700	900
Marylebone Station*	200			25	50	100	200	
Bow Street	180	100	14	70	200	550	750	950
Community Chest								
Marlborough Street	180	100	14	70	200	550	750	950

Table D.1 (Continued)

Square Name	Book Cost	Development Cost	Rent - 0 houses	1	2	3	4	Hotel
Vine Street	200	100	16	80	220	600	800	1,000
Free Parking								
Strand	220	150	18	90	250	700	875	1,050
Chance								
Fleet Street	220	150	18	90	250	700	875	1,050
Trafalgar Square	240	150	20	100	300	750	925	1,100
Fenchurch Street*	200			25	50	100	200	
Leicester Square	260	150	22	110	330	800	975	1,150
Coventry Street	260	150	22	110	330	800	975	1,150
Water Works**	150							
Piccadilly	280	150	24	120	360	850	1,025	1,200
Go To Jail								
Regent Street	300	200	26	130	390	900	1,100	1,275
Oxford Street	300	200	26	130	390	900	1,100	1,275
Community Chest								
Bond Street	320	200	28	150	450	1,000	1,200	1,400
Liverpool St. Station*	200			25	50	100	200	
Chance								
Park Lane	350	200	35	175	500	1,100	1,300	1,500
Super Tax								
Mayfair	400	200	50	200	600	1,400	1,700	2,000

* For Railway Stations, rent receivable is determined by the number of Railway Station title deeds a player owns rather than the number of houses developed.

** For Utility, rent receivable is determined by the number of Utility title deeds a player owns and the dice roll of the player in turn.
If player A owns one Utility deed and player B rolls 6 to land on that deed space, player B owes player A GBP 6 x 4 = GBP 24.
If player A owns both Utility deeds and player B rolls 6 to land on that deed space, player B owes player A GBP 6 x 10 = GBP 60.

Appendix 1

Now that students may have identified what methods exist and the different ways in which those methods can arise, they can be prompted with a more critical analysis of how to assess which methods are the best for winning the game. Questions in Table 7.12 will help structure the thought process amongst students (Tables 7.13 to 7.17).

Students can be prompted if needed to collectively be able to come up with the methods listed in Tables 7.13 to 7.16 to answer question 1.

Table 7.12 Complex Methods of Increasing Wealth Questions

Question No	Question
1	For each of the methods of increasing a player's wealth in the game, consider the advantages and disadvantages of each.
2	Whilst considering a framework where the primary objective in the game is to bankrupt other players and the secondary objective is to have enough wealth to survive several turns in the game, consider which wealth-increasing methods achieve either of these objectives.

Table 7.13 Advantages/Disadvantages of Passing "Go"

Advantages	Disadvantages
No expenditure/investment necessary	Income is limited to GBP 200 each time and cannot be increased
Probability of occurring is inevitable	Frequency of income is comparatively low owing to dependency on going around the board once each time

Table 7.14 Advantages/Disadvantages of Rent

Advantages	Disadvantages
Scalable investment capable of forcing players into bankruptcy	Large initial capital expenditure necessary
Frequency of occurring is comparatively high as players can own multiple title deeds and income can be earned several times in round of the board	Ongoing expenditure necessary in houses/hotels to scale rental value of properties
	Requires ownership of entire title deed groups to enable house/hotel development

Table 7.15 Advantages/Disadvantages of Chance/Community Chest

Advantages	Disadvantages
No investment expenditure required	Income amount is limited to GBP 200 for certain cards.
	Low probability of occurring and entirely dependent on dice roll.
	Sometimes these cards require players to pay out rather than receiving income.

Table 7.16 Advantages/Disadvantages of Trading

Advantages	Disadvantages
Can be initiated at any point in the game without dependency on dice roll	Requires cooperation from other players
Can be used strategically to generate large amounts of cash if demand on a particular property is high enough	

Table 7.17 Wealth Method and Achieving Game Objectives

Method	Shorthand	Primary Objective (Bankrupting Other Players) Achieved?	Secondary Objective (Surviving Your Turn in the Game) Achieved?
1	Passing "Go"	No	Yes
2	Rent	Yes*	Yes
3	Chance/Community Chest	No	Yes
4	Trading	No	Yes

* Collecting rent from other players is arguably the only method which has a high enough probability of bankrupting other players. This is largely because rental amounts receivable can be scaled large enough to extract money fast enough to prevent the paying player from replenishing their wealth via the random events in time to avoid bankruptcy.

Students can be prompted if needed to collectively be able to come up with the methods listed in Table 7.17 to answer question 2.

Appendix 2
Challenging Metric Selection: Traditional and Enhanced

Once students correctly identify the items defined, you may pose the question of what metrics are effective at measuring the strength of following a particular option when faced with a decision. Examples may include (Table 7.18):

Table 7.18 Challenging Metric Selection Questions

Question No	Question
1	When a player lands on a specific board space (and the title deed is not otherwise owned by another player), should they purchase the property?
2	When a player already owns a complete set of properties (which enables them to develop houses and hotels), should they invest in developing houses/hotels?
3	When other players own desired properties, should the player make a bid to purchase them?

Traditional Metric Selection

All these decisions can be based on a projected outcome – namely, an increase of the metric defined. Students may at first suggest that the primary metric to use is player wealth (measured in cash and book value of properties; Table 7.19).

Example 1

Taking question 1 as an example, if there are four players (A, B, C and D) and player A rolls 7 on the dice to land on the Angel Islington, should they purchase it for GBP 100? The thought process might be to compare the GBP 100 against the expected benefit in rental receipts.

With three other players sitting on the "Go" square, each with a 16.7% probability of landing on the Angel Islington space, the aggregate projected rental receipts are calculated in Table 7.19.

This means player A expects to recover GBP 3 of their initial GBP 100 investment, i.e., a 3% return on investment on one lap of the board (Table 7.20).

Example 2

Taking question 2 from the table as an example, if there are six players (A, B, C, D, E, F) all currently sitting on the "Go" square and assuming hypothetically that player A already owns two group title deeds (the Angel Islington and Euston Road), and player A rolls 9 to land on Pentonville Road. Should

Table 7.19 Calculating Expected Rental Receipt Value

Player	Probability of Landing on Space	Rental Value (Assuming 0 Houses, Player A Does Not Own Whole Set and Other Players Land on Space)	Expected Rental Receipt Without Knowing Dice Rolls of Players B, C and D
B	16.7%	6	1
C	16.7%	6	1
D	16.7%	6	1
Total			3

Table 7.20 Calculating Rental Receipt Value from Group of Title Deeds

Player	Probability of Landing on Space	Rental Value (Assuming 0 Houses, Player A Owns Whole Set and Other Players Land on Space)	Expected Rental Receipt without Knowing Dice Rolls of Players B, C and D
B	11.1%	40	4.4
C	11.1%	40	4.4
D	11.1%	40	4.4
E	11.1%	40	4.4
F	11.1%	40	4.4
Total			22

player A invest GBP 120 to complete the title deed group and should they invest an additional GBP 150 to build one house on each property space?

The aggregate projected rental receipts are calculated in Table 7.20.

This means player A expects to recover GBP 22 of their GBP 270 investment (GBP 120 to purchase Pentonville Road and 3 x GBP 50 to purchase one house on each property in that group) – i.e., an 8% return on investment on one lap of the board.

Enhanced Metric Selection

In practice, the game only ends when all other players are bankrupt. This in turn should lead to a discussion about whether increasing personal wealth is the same as bankrupting opposing players (see Section 3.1 for the game objective).

Pose the question "is it worth spending GBP 200 of my own money to make an opponent lose GBP 100?"

If this scenario arises at the beginning of the game, then it is unlikely to be a favourable thing to do. However, if this scenario exists in the end game – i.e., spending GBP 200 will cause your opponent to lose GBP 100 on their next turn and cause them bankruptcy – then perhaps it is worth doing.

Appendix 3

Multiple Roll Dice Probability Distribution

The model described in single roll dice only goes as far as computing the probability of an outcome over one roll of both dice. In practice, players might roll identical values on the dice ('doubles') and be granted another turn (Table 7.21).

The probability distribution model could theoretically be extended beyond the possibilities shown and the outcome column is capped at 35 representing the furthest a player can travel on the board without rolling three doubles and ending up in jail (Table 7.22).

Table 7.21 Multiple Roll Dice Probability Questions

Question No	Question
1	In what circumstances does a player get granted more than one roll of the dice?
2	How probable is it that a player will go to jail after rolling doubles three times consecutively?

Table 7.22 Computing Probability Distribution Questions

Question	Disadvantages
1	Assuming player position on the board is known, can you predict with more accuracy which spaces are more likely to be landed on?"

Appendix 4

Computing Probability Distribution

Students may be challenged to develop a mathematical expression which predicts probability of landing on a particular square number given a particular starting square. One possible way of expressing this is given in the following expression.

$$P(n \mid x) = A + B + C + D$$

- P is the probability of landing on square number 'n', given a starting position of square number 'x'.
- A is the probability element represented by rolling the required numbers on the dice roll. This must take into account the possibility of rolling doubles and therefore rolling the dice again. Refer to Section 5.1.2 on how to go about calculating this.
- B is the probability element represented by being sent to square number 'n' because of first landing on another square number where the game instructions dictate the player must move to square number 'n'. In practice, this only happens when players land on square number 31 ("Go to Jail") and are sent to square number 11 ("Jail").
- C is the probability element represented by being forced onto square 'n' as a result of rolling three doubles in a row. In practice, square number 'n' here will always be 11 ("Jail").
- D is the probability element represented by being forced onto square 'n' as a result of a Chance or Community Chest card instructing to do so (Tables 7.23 and 7.24).

Proving Probability Distribution

Table 7.23 Complex Methods of Proving Probability Distribution Questions

Question No	Question
1	Can you build a repetitive simulation which performs 10,000 dice rolls and tracks the frequency of landing on each board space?
2	What would the pseudo-algorithm look like in the form of a flow chart?

Table 7.24 Using Probability Distribution Advantageously Questions

Question No	Question
1	Which space on the board appears to be the most frequented space?
2	Can you visualise the results in a bar graph distribution?

Developing a Strategy to Play Monopoly™ 77

Using Probability Distribution Advantageously

You may provide them with Figure 7.3 as an illustrative example but ensure they understand the values presented in the figure are arbitrary and should be re-calculated using whatever method they choose to explore.

Board Space Number Frequency Distribution

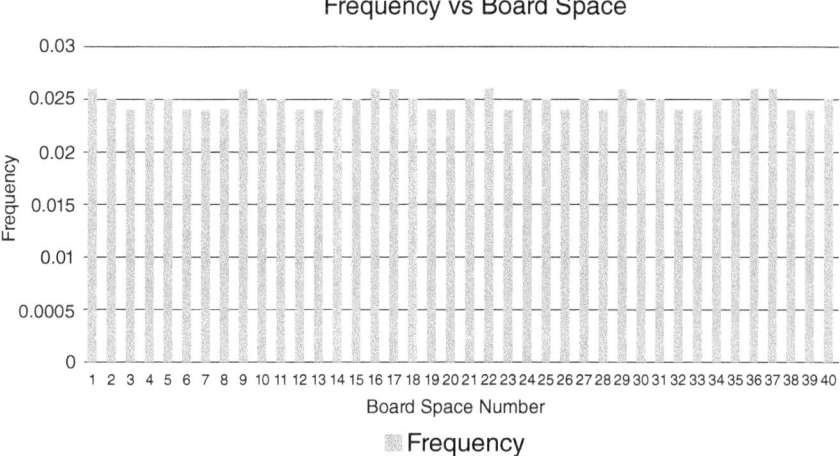

Figure 7.3 Board space number frequency distribution.

Appendix 5

A more complex algorithm in Figure 7.4 enables the player to reject the purchase offer even if sufficient cash is available. The question of whether a particular property enhances an existing portfolio is a matter of degree and setting appropriate minimum thresholds.

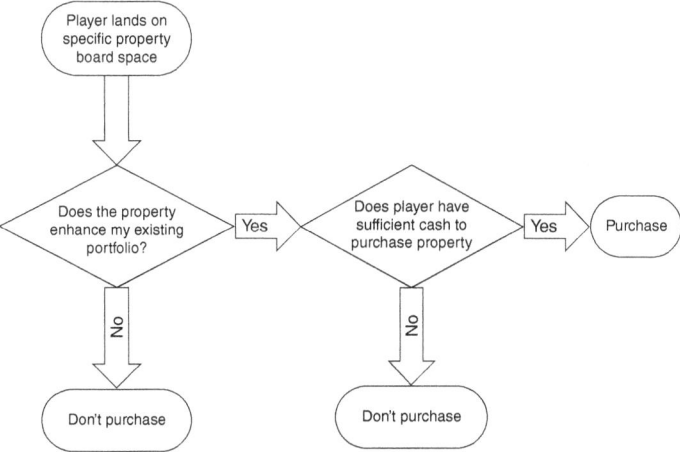

Figure 7.4 Moderate property purchase flow diagram.

Moderate Property Purchase Algorithm

Students may wish to evaluate the cost-benefit of each purchasing decision. Questions to provoke thought are outlined in Table 7.25:

Table 7.25 Moderate Property Purchase Questions

Question No	Question
1	How would you decide whether a new property enhances a player's existing portfolio? On the basis that an entire property set (e.g., three title deeds of the same colour) have a higher income potential from rent than each one in isolation, should players be willing to pay a premium for properties that help them complete a set?
2	If properties are automatically auctioned to the highest bidder if the player who landed on the space chooses not to purchase it, then how much would other players be willing to bid to buy the property in question? Would this depend on their existing portfolio?
3	Should the decision to purchase a property be influenced by trying to deprive a particular player from completing a full set of properties?
4	How would you calculate a break-even period when purchasing a property? Is there a specific amount of time you would expect the property to return the initial sum invested based on predicted probability of other players landing on that space?

Appendix 6

Purchasing from other players: which properties to buy/sell, how much to pay/receive for the property.

Which Properties Should I Buy or Sell?

A player's desire to purchase a property is enhanced if they already own other properties in that set. Questions to provoke thought are outlined in Tables 7.26 and 7.27:

Table 7.26 Which Properties Should I Buy/Sell Questions

Question No	Question
1	How do I define a single method for ranking each property's desirability?
2	Should certain property types be favoured over others based on their ability to be developed with houses/hotels vs. other properties like utilities and train stations?
3	How many properties of a set should I already own to establish desire in purchasing the remaining properties?
4	If a quantitative measure of desirability was established, should a low measure of that quantity constitute a desire to sell the property?
5	Should players' positions on the board be taken into account when measuring desirability to buy/sell a property? Should a player try to purchase a property immediately before they expect other players to land on it, and can this be done accurately using the probability distribution previously established?
6	Can you develop a mathematical expression which will compute a value that can be compared with a threshold limit where exceeding the threshold means a positive decision and not exceeding the decision means a negative decision?
7	When setting a threshold value for question 6, should the threshold have a fixed value or should it also evolve as the game progresses?

Table 7.27 Advantages/Disadvantages of Mathematical Expression

Advantages	Disadvantages
Relatively simple to compute	Will always result in zero value if the player does not already own the first property in the set

Students may come up with variations of the following expression and should debate the advantages and disadvantages of their expression.

$$D = f\left\{\frac{n}{N} \times E(r)\right\}$$

Where
 n = number of properties already owned in set
 N = maximum number of properties belonging to that set
 $E(r)$ = expected rent from one round of dice rolls from each player if property were purchased immediately

Table 7.28 How Much to Pay/Receive for a Property Questions

Question No	Question
1	What parameters should feed into a decision-making framework to establish a suitable purchase price?
2	Should inflation be taken into account? As players pass the Go space more and more, the money supply in the game increases and should this justify being able to charge a higher price for a specific property?
3	If player A already owns two properties from a coloured set, and they are seeking to purchase the remaining property from player B, should player B charge them a premium to complete the set compared with if player B were selling to another player who didn't already own the other properties within that set?

How Much Should I Pay/Receive for This Property?

When purchasing properties from other players, the traditional book value of the property set by the game rules is no longer applicable to the transaction because the purchase price is subject to a mutual agreement between players (Table 7.28).

Note

1 Classic Monopoly Rules published at: https://www.hasbro.com/common/instruct/00009.pdf.

8 Reclamation
Game-Based Critical Re-thinking of Historical First and Bests

Chiedza Mutsaka Skyum and Puja Singh

8.1 Overview

Never has there been a stronger call to action for teachers of history, social sciences and international relations (IR) to challenge the history of the world as it has been told for centuries. Much of today's lack of equity and systemic oppression of certain races, sects and populations arises from the actions of countries and their people, done in the name of sovereignty, nation building and prosperity. Erasure, exclusion and mistellings in history, in textbooks and even in current news articles continues to this day.

Despite the availability of an abundance of information on the making of the world we have inherited, a significant part of the global population remains unaware and unable to deter from the 'oppressionist' versions of 'firsts' and 'bests' in innovation, discovery, science and the arts that have been printed and reprinted in textbooks that are lobbied to portray a constructed truth. This chapter aims to explore a learning tool that challenges such norms and examines this erasure of histories and achievements.

DOI: 10.4324/9781003230120-8

The researchers believe that a game-based critical examination and practice in social sciences will not only enable learners to widen their narrow boundaries[1] but also immerse themselves in using critical theory to dismantle the constructed truth and dive into all angles, perspectives and narratives of parties and people involved and help learners to gain transferrable questioning skills and habits that can always find room to bring to light the voices, actions, discoveries, inventions and wins of groups that have long been neglected (hooks 1994).

Through the use of game-based learning and inquiry-based exploration, through 'aha' moments and emotional and empathic engagement, learners can experience true liberatory education. A critical re-thinking and a necessarily humane contextualisation of events should not only be encouraged but demanded if education is going to play a part in ensuring an equitable future. With skills learned in this game, learners can read textbooks with a critical eye and expand to use their questioning skills even when reading the news, blogs online or when being told a story.

From a cognitive perspective,[2] games are considered to be motivational environments that are likely to require excess amounts of information to be processed by the learner (Shute et al. 2014). This game-based approach to critical re-thinking of a specific caveat of history and its cognitive impact can be rationalised based on relevant theory. The parameters of cognitive foundations[3] of game-based design are considered to be situatedness of learning, transfer of learning, scaffolding and feedback, dynamic assessment, information design, interaction design and gestures and movement (Plass et al. 2015).

The overall subject being used in the game is social sciences – more specifically history and IR. The two game designers are both teachers of IR, political science and history, one in European and Asian university classrooms and the other in African university classrooms. They share a responsibility towards creating consciousness-raising learning experiences and critical pedagogy[4] (Fobes and Kaufman 2008). Based on this, the game fulfils the first parameter of cognitive foundations of game design: situatedness of learning.

The game provides ample contextual and meaningful information with references and clues. The understanding of erasure, exclusion and mistelling of history after playing the game, provides the learners with the data and context that allows them to approach higher levels of abstractions when confronted with other information relevant to the topics and issues that the various questions of the game covers. This abstraction of how power and politics might have resulted in the wrong portrayal of people, places, countries and contexts adds a layer of critical inquiry (CI) that is lacking in current education contexts. As such, the game fulfils the second parameter of cognitive game-based learning: transfer of learning.

The third parameter of cognitive foundations of game development, scaffolding and feedback, is an important design feature of this game. The clues provided not only act as scaffolding for the learners but also support the abstraction process of the learner's critical inquiry into history as it is told in books and stories. The CI cards in the game design provide ample opportunity for not only feedback but the deconstruction of current abstractions in the learner's mind. This not only contributes to addressing biases but also enhances positive and open communication of the wrong abstractions and the deconstruction of it.

The card and clues format of the game adheres to the fourth parameter: information design. The simple card format provides information whilst not contributing to the cognitive load that game designers are concerned about. These specific CI skills in this game have been identified as necessary in classrooms where the majority of textbooks and learning materials have been penned in Europe or the USA and questions arise amongst students. It invites questioning and contextualising and hence transforming knowledge[5] instead of simple consumption of it (Giroux 2011). Critical pedagogy,[6] a teaching approach which guides students in questioning power structures and challenging the beliefs and known dominating practices finds a home in these classrooms (Freire 1972). The game provides a structure and a pathway for this question to be not only fun and engaging[7] but also habit-forming.

The last parameter, interaction design is facilitated by the CI cards and the communicative aspects of the game. Through the rigorous process of CI, learners arrive at new ways of seeing and acting that allow them to examine current and past practices of knowledge production. This dialogue, encouraged by the CI cards, is a means to help learners challenge their assumptions and, if they find them wanting, to change them. They gain increased awareness of the complex set of interactions between different groups over time. The cards invoke the learning principles under CI Theory and the deconstruction of their previous assumptions/knowledge or abstraction and the communication that occurs during the process adheres to Transformative Learning Theory. The scaffolded questioning method in this game helps learners to acquire questioning and CI skills that are transferable life skills.

In describing his Transformative Learning Theory, Mezirow[8] explains that "transformative learning is perspective transformation, a paradigm shift, whereby we critically examine our prior interpretations and assumptions to form new meaning" (Mezirow 2003).

Through practice, learners demonstrate[9] how to deconstruct and disrupt the status quo by confronting stereotypes, biases, prejudices and assumptions (Bermúdez 2015). This is something that they may find themselves using in other classrooms, in the workplace, when reading the news, a book or an online article. They can use the same questioning methods acquired in the game to confront the stances of politicians they are considering voting for or against, to research non-governmental organisations or companies they are considering donating or working for. The learner ceases to be a passive consumer of what they read but instead advances to internalise these CI skills.

Some of the examples given here in this chapter demonstrate how this game can actually be used in multiple different fields. It can be adapted for a scientific classroom; it can be used in the public sector when drafting policies that affect diverse groups; it can be used for company team-building to build greater critical consciousness amongst employees in a team-building activity; it can be used by human resources departments in understanding how to establish an equitable workplace environment.

In moving from lecturing and banking[10] methods of teaching in social sciences, this CI game encourages the eradication of the teacher-student contradiction whereby the teacher teaches and the learners are taught; the teacher knows everything and the learners know nothing; the teacher talks and the learners listen; the teacher is the subject and the learners are mere objects. Learners in this game are encouraged by their teachers to engage in problem-posing dialogue. This discourse becomes central to making meaning because learning is a social process (Mezirow 2003).

The skills acquired go beyond this game, beyond the classroom, striving for real praxis in other subjects and in daily life, learners examine and reflect upon the social world in order to transform it. This type of transformative learning enables them to apply their learning in unexpected situations, thus enhancing its place in all forms of university and adult education.

8.2 Games Details

8.2.1 Key Skills

CI, asking questions, challenging dominant perspectives, social constructivism

8.2.2 Group Size

From two to an unlimited number of players

8.2.3 Time

From 30 minutes to unlimited amounts of time. The recommended minimum time frame of 30 minutes is quoted on the assumption that there should be a fortifying/scaffolded deep thinking and CI

8.2.4 Purpose (Learning Objectives)

1. Demonstrate the ability to ask critical, reflective and disruptive questions. The game posits an emphasis on how the answers came to be a certain place or country in the player's heads than what the answer is or whether it is correct or not. To fully explore the dominant perspectives that cloud our ways of thinking, the CI cards should be used to ask critical, reflective and disruptive questions.

2. Confront systematic stereotypes, biases and assumptions. Instead of banking stereotypes, biases and assumptions as normal, logical or socially transposed, the CI cards are designed to enable a deeper thinking into why and how we have succumbed to such social conditioning.
3. Articulate, critique and support arguments with compelling and sound reasoning. The CI cards and the format of the game together will promote the articulation of thoughts and narratives, allow students to critique each other's narratives in a non-threatening and constructive game format and will encourage players to apply reason and logic to formation of arguments in a storytelling and creative way.
4. Revise a point of view in response to new arguments and information. In a game-based environment, individuals can find it easier to change points of view and take in new evidence and information to change perspectives and thoughts much more easily than in real life. The consequences and implication to self are perceived to be much less detrimental in a game environment.

8.2.5 Preparation and Setup

The game can be played by two people or in a group with one person as the initiator. Team formation can also be suggested but will not necessarily change the play or the scoring.

- Room –
    - If face-to-face, each group only needs to be seated around a shared table.
    - If virtual, the scorekeeper or initiator must share their screen with the CI game cards.
    - If virtual, players can be encouraged to type their answers on the chat box of the call.
- Tech –
    - If face-to-face, no tech required
    - If virtual, game players should be able to have both video and audio so that they can see the game cards shared on the screen of the game master.

8.2.6 Guidance

Players should be encouraged to be forthcoming and honest to their first thoughts and intuition. It should be established that wrong answers are an opportunity for deeper thinking and reflection.

Players should also be made to understand the importance of exposing deeply rooted systemic thinking, biases and stereotypes in the social constructivist process.

8.2.7 Instructions

8.2.7.1 Player Roles

- Initiator
  - The person asking the 'question' which can be an Invention, a Product or a Process (using an IPP card) shall be the initiator. As the initiator, this person (or a representative of a team if teams are formed) will be responsible for fostering a positive and encouraging learning environment and triggering the right questions and narrative to induce CI.
  - After each round, the initiator role will change to another Player.
- Scorekeeper According to the Score
  - This role can be played by the initiator or by a second person in each round. The job of the scorekeeper is to simply keep scores according to the scoring sheet instructions.
- Player Group
  - The rest of the participants are players. The IPP question is posed to all. All must answer the guessing question from the IPP cards, but the second level of the game involving the CI cards should be answered by one player at a time.

8.2.7.2 Types of Cards

A. IPP card: *See Material 1*
   Initiators are pre-planned to create these cards, and the accompanying three clues will help players guess where the IPP was first discovered/invented.
B. CI card: *See Material 2*

   There are four categories of CI cards

   A. Reasoning
   B. Perspective
   C. Sceptic
   D. System

8.2.7.3 Game Phase 1: Discovery

Step 1: Choosing the IPP card and first impression guess

- **Initiator** will lay or hold the IPP cards for the players to choose. Lay or hold the cards with the front side of the card facing the players so they cannot see the clues and the answer written on the back side (Figure 8.1).

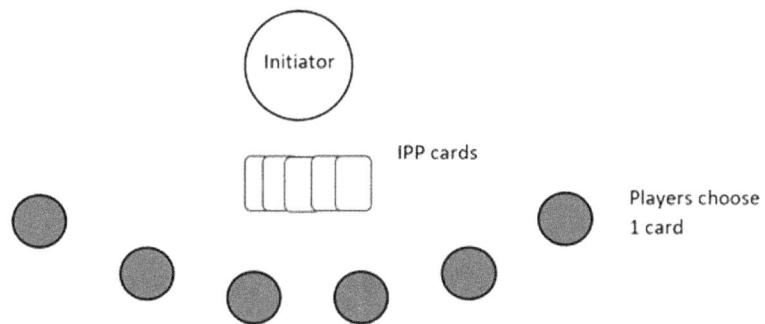

Figure 8.1 Setup for choosing IPP cards.

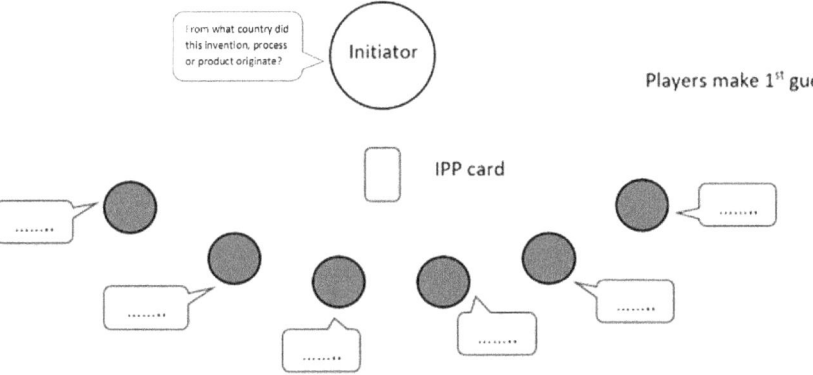

Figure 8.2 Setup for asking questions and first guesses.

After the players pick a card, ask them to guess which country the invention/product or process on the IPP cards originated from (Figure 8.2).

- If they guess right on the first attempt, pick a new card and start again (Player that guesses right gets 5 points – **Scorekeeper** logs all scores).
- If they guess wrong, each player should note down the countries they guess for later and move to Step 2.

Step 2: Guessing clues
- Think about and give any three clues to assist the players in guessing which country it was discovered/invented in first (Figure 8.3).
  - If a player guesses after the first clue, they get 3 points.
  - If a player guesses after the second clue, they get 2 points.
  - If a player only guesses after the third clue, they get 1 point.

Step 3: The big reveal

Initiator delivers the answer of which country it is actually from.

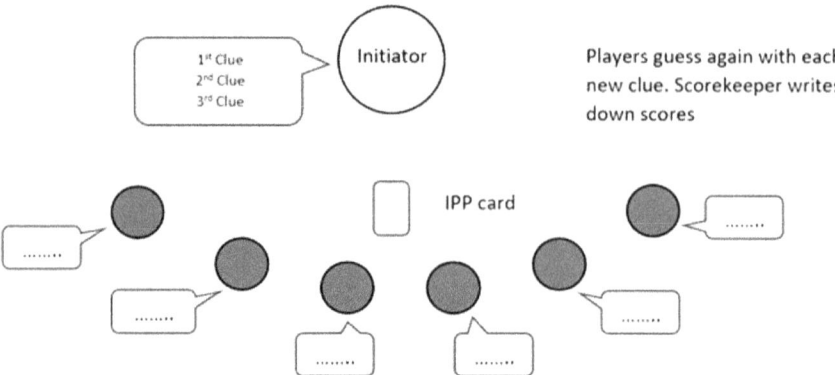

Figure 8.3 Setup for giving clues.

8.2.7.4 Game Phase 2: CI

Step 4: CI

After it has been revealed what the correct answer is and all scores have been tallied for that round, the initiator can approach the second part of the game, which is the CI section. Depending on the time available, the initiator can pursue one of the following options:

Option A (plenty of time for discussion in each round):
Progress together through all four categories of CI cards one category at a time.

Initiator asks players to choose and explain which card most represents their process towards guessing a particular country. The initiator can pick on specific players or can go around the table in order. It is the turn of the initiator of the round to take the lead in the discussion and decide which questions will make for a rich discussion (Figure 8.4).

For example:

- Which Reasoning CI card best explains why you guessed your first answer?
- Which Perspective CI card best explains why you guessed your second answer?
- Which Sceptic CI card best explains why you guessed your third answer?
- Which System CI card can spark debate on explaining why you guessed your first answer?

Example follow-up questions to enrich discussion can include the following:

- What from the first clue led you to answer that country as you guess? Which card would you choose to represent that line of thinking?
- The second clue was about _____. Which system card can we use for explaining why many of you had this answer after the second clue?

Reclamation 89

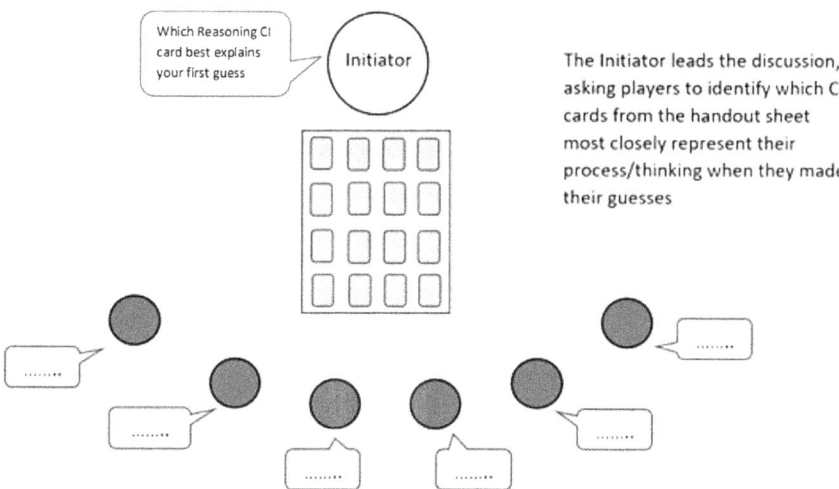

Figure 8.4 Setup for initiating discussion.

Option B (limited time):
If time is limited, do one CI card category per round so that the players have time to progress to more guessing. The initiator can choose one category of CI cards to ask about that can lead to a discussion in their round and in the following rounds, the next initiators can then use the other categories.

Questions and follow-up questions can follow the same line as Option A.
After this step is complete, Return to Step 1 with a new initiator.

8.2.8 Debrief

What was the most challenging part of the game?
What was the most rewarding part of the game?
What are you curious about?
What did you learn about yourself?
In what activities/scenarios in your life do you see yourself remembering the CI cards and putting CI skills to use?

8.2.9 Handouts and Material

Material 1: IPP cards printed and cut out.
Material 2: One-page printout of the CI cards.

8.2.9.1 Material 1: IPP Card

Initiators are pre-planned to create these cards and the accompanying three clues that will help players guess where the IPP was first discovered/invented. IPP card front and back side:

Copyright material from Hirani & Varin 2003, *Supporting Adult Learners through Games and Interactive Teaching*, Routledge

Photography

Clue 1: A former popular Football player from this Country was playing for the FC Barcelona.
Clue 2: Its street festival is the most popular among tourists.
Clue 3: The Country Contains an irreplaceable amount of natural resources.

Photography
Brazil

Hércules Florence, a French-Brazilian inventor, is considered one of the pioneers of photography, developing a photograph some three years before Louis Daguerre.

CAT Scan

Clue 1: This country is the only one to have hosted the Football, Cricket and Rugby World Cups.
Clue 2: It is the only country in the world that has voluntarily abandoned a nuclear weapons program
Clue 3: It is the country with the most Official languages (11)

CAT Scan
South Africa

In November 1975, South African Physicist and inventor Robert Ledley invented a mathematical technique in which X-ray source and electronic detectors could be rotated around a body.

Mathematics

Clue 1: This country is one of the top oil producers in the world.
Clue 2: After a military embargo, this country switched from a dictatorship to a federal government.
Clue 3: This country is home of the world's earliest form of writing.

Mathematics
Iraq

The earliest evidence of written mathematics dates to the ancient Sumerians, who built the earliest civilization in Mesopotamia. They developed a complex system of metrology from 3000 BC.

Emojis

Clue 1: Life expectancy in this country is the highest in the world.
Clue 2: A particular spring flower attracts millions of tourists to this country.
Clue 3: Its history boasts the first superheroes.

Emojis
Japan

Shigetaka Kurita created the first emoji in 1999, he had to work within a grid measuring 12 by 12 pixels.

Copyright material from Hirani & Varin 2003, *Supporting Adult Learners through Games and Interactive Teaching*, Routledge

Contraceptive Pill Clue 1: Your favorite alcoholic drink for crazy partying is brewed from a plant that grows in this country. Clue 2: A popular festival celebrating dead people has its origin here. Clue 3: Its beaches are most popular for Spring Break vacationers.	**Contraceptive Pill** **Mexico** Mexican chemist Luis E. Miramontes invented the first oral contraceptive pill in 1956.
Democracy Clue 1: A city in this country is considered the wettest inhabited place in the world. Clue 2: Diamonds were first mined in this country. Clue 3: It the second largest English-speaking country in the world	**Democracy** **India** The Republic of Vashali, situated in today's India, was a democratic republic a century before Athens in Greece.
Coffee Clue 1: This country has 13 and not 12 months to a year. Clue 2: It is considered the birthplace of the Rastafarian culture. Clue 3: The oldest hominid skeleton was found in this country.	**Coffee** **Ethiopia** Coffee has grown in the wild in this country since the 10th Century BC.
Paper Money Clue 1: This country's new year celebrations last 15 days. Clue 2: It has the biggest population speaking one language in the world. Clue 3: A 2400-year-old pot of soup was unearthed here.	**Paper Money** **China** Paper money has been used in China since 8 or 9th Century AD as an exchange certificate.

Copyright material from Hirani & Varin 2003, *Supporting Adult Learners through Games and Interactive Teaching*, Routledge

MP3	MP3 South Korea
Clue 1: This country has the fastest internet in the world. Clue 2: Its popular music has the biggest fan following in the world. Clue 3: People of this country are already 1 year old when they are born.	MP3 files were first developed here in 1997 by Digital Cast & Saehan.
Anesthesia	**Anesthesia Spain**
Clue 1: Nudity is legal in this country. Clue 2: The first novel was written in its language. Clue 3: It is the home of world's second most widely spoken language.	Al-Zahrawi in the 10th century describes its usage in his book, Method of Medicine.

8.2.9.2 Material 2: CI Cards

There are four categories of CI cards:

A. Reasoning
B. Perspective
C. Sceptic
D. System

   a. **Reasoning** CI Cards

Copyright material from Hirani & Varin 2003, *Supporting Adult Learners through Games and Interactive Teaching*, Routledge

b. **Perspective** CI Cards

| Ethnicity / Race | Class/ Socioeconomic Status | History / Geopolitics | Society / Media |

c. **Sceptic** CI Cards

| Stereotype | Bias | Assumption | Prejudice |

d. **System** CI Cards

| Who is a friend? | Who is a foe? | Who has got the power? | Who is missing? |

8.3 Adaptation of the Games to a Different Context

This game can be used in diverse contexts. Instead of using Inventions/ Products, for the IPP cards, a teacher can compile

- a list of facts from history or short descriptions of political or scientific events
- a list of previous winners of sporting events around the world and ask what country they originated from

Copyright material from Hirani & Varin 2003, *Supporting Adult Learners through Games and Interactive Teaching*, Routledge

- a list of Nobel prize winners and what they won for and ask where they are from
- a list of information technology and computer science inventions
- a list of fashion designers' famous looks, and learners can guess the origin of the inspiration for these looks

The CI cards are definitely the most versatile – any teacher should be able to use these cards in any classroom to ask learners to attempt to categorise their thinking process and rationale when answering questions in the classroom. It is important for learners to have that self-awareness of their own biases, assumptions, stereotypes and prejudices.

Notes

1 "Multiculturalism compels educators to recognize the narrow boundaries that have shaped the way knowledge is shared in the classroom. It forces us all to recognise our complicity in accepting and perpetuating biases of any kind" (hooks 1994).
2 "Games are considered either environments that are motivating but likely to require excess amounts of information to be processed by the learner" (Shute et al. 2014).
3 The rationale on the validation of the game's contribution to cognitive foundation of learning is based on the work of Plass et al. (2015).
4 "The distinguishing feature of critical pedagogy is that it is both a form of practice and a form of action. Critical pedagogy does not only tell us how to teach and learn—much less what to teach and learn; rather, it also implores us to use our teaching and learning to effect positive social change" (Fobes and Kaufman 2008).
5 "Critical pedagogy becomes a project that stresses the need for teachers and students to actively transform knowledge rather than simply consume it" (Giroux 2011).
6 Critical pedagogy draws on the work of many educationalists, but mainly Brazilian Paulo Freire (1972), Henry Giroux (2011) and bell hooks (1994), who advocates around what she called engaged pedagogy.
7 The game was piloted on Tuesday 22 September 2020 with 11 undergraduate social sciences students from around the world in a virtual classroom setting using Zoom
[Student nationalities: Germany (1), Nigeria (1), the Netherlands (1), Romania (3), Rwanda (2), Sierra Leone (1), Zimbabwe (1)]. Quotes from student feedback follow:

> "I think it was surprising how much we could learn from a simple set of cards in a short period of time. If I can remember those cards, I can use them in my other classwork and beyond".
> "I think the game has potential and was nice to do, the whole intention is good practice and an effective way of learning perspectives and can be valuable".
> "It was fun!"
> "It really made me think differently about how quickly my mind went to the richer countries for guessing first. I am programmed for it".

8 Jack Mezirow was an American sociologist of continuing education at Teachers College, Columbia University. He lays out ten phases of Transformative Learning in his theory: (1) a disorienting dilemma, (2) self-examination of assumptions, (3) critical reflection on assumptions, (4) recognition of dissatisfaction, (5) exploration of alternatives, (6) plan for action, (7) acquisition of new knowledge, (8) experimentation with roles, (9) competence building and (10) reintegration into life on the basis of new perspectives. The authors do not believe that all of these phases will be reached as is in this game but that the learners will find themselves going through a more rapid transformational cognitive process.
9 Inspired by Bermúdez (2015), whose article, "Four Tools for Critical Inquiry in History, Social Studies, and Civic Education" recognises the struggle that educators face in translating "general definitions of critical thinking into specific pedagogical tools to plan learning activities and to observe and interpret student work in these subjects" (Bermudez 2015). Bermudez's 4 CI tools are problem posing, reflective scepticism, multiperspectivity and systemic thinking. These four tools are what the researchers adapted to inspire the 4 CI card categories.
10 The banking concept in education is one explored by Paulo Freire in his 1972 book *Pedagogy of the Oppressed*, where he posits that the traditional method of education is one where metaphorically, the students are containers, 'banks' into which the teachers merely make deposits of information.

Bibliography

Bermúdez, Á. (2015). Four tools for critical inquiry in history, social studies, and civic education. *Revista de Estudios Sociales No. 35*, 52(52), pp. 102–18.

Fobes, C., and Kaufman, P. (2008). Critical pedagogy in the sociology classroom: Challenges and concerns. *Teaching Sociology*, 36(1), pp. 26–33.

Freire, P. (1972). *Pedagogy of the oppressed*. New York: Herder and Herder.

Giroux, H. A. (2011). *On critical pedagogy*. New York: Continuum International Publishing Group.

hooks, bell. (1994). *Teaching to transgress: Education as the practice of freedom*. New York: Routledge.

Mezirow, J. (2003). Transformative learning as discourse. *Journal of Transformative Education*, 1(1), pp. 58–63.

Plass, J., Homer, B., and Kinzer, C. (2015). Foundations of game based learning. *Educational Psychologist*, 50(4), pp. 258–83.

Shute, V., Ventura, M., and Ke, F. (2014). The power of play: The effects of portal 2 and lumosity on cognitive and noncognitive skills. *Computers & Education*, 80, pp. 58–67.

9 Using Role-Play to Understand the Impacts of Social Media through Action Research

Sequoyah Wharton

9.1 Overview

Active learning describes any instructional practice that engages students in learning, requiring them to complete and reflect on meaningful learning activities (Prince 2004). Increasingly, researchers and educators view active learning as a valuable tool for improving student engagement, motivation, and autonomy (Planander 2013). Active learning stands in contrast to traditional pedagogical models in which students passively receive information from teachers, as it requires students to become active participants in the learning process (Minhas et al. 2012). Educators can incorporate different types of active learning into classroom curriculum, including collaborative learning, cooperative learning, and problem-based learning (Prince 2004). Role-play is an interesting but underutilized form of collaborative and cooperative active learning, which provides the basis of this activity.

DOI: 10.4324/9781003230120-9

Role-play fosters high levels of engagement and autonomy, and has been found to offer several academic benefits. For example, research indicates role-play helps students develop deeper understandings of topics, stimulates interest, and may be more efficient in helping students absorb and retain information (McCarthy and Anderson 1999; Rao and Stupans 2012; Ruhanen 2005). As a form of active learning, role-play is also a valuable tool for scaffolding and catering to students' different learning needs (Planander 2013).

Existing studies on role-play indicate widespread use in language learning classrooms and higher education. For example, Shapiro and Leopold (2012) described the benefits of role-play activities in "Teaching English as a Second Language" classrooms. Rahman and Maarof (2018) found role-play significantly improved ESL learners' oral communication skills. Latif et al. (2018) reported that role-play enhanced medical students' communication and clinical skills. While less research exists on role-play in primary and secondary classrooms, teachers should consider this a valuable pedagogical strategy, especially for introducing students to complex topics such as action research. Kurt Lewin (1946) coined the term *action research* to describe comparative research on the conditions and effects of various phenomena that lead to social action. Action research is a form of investigation in which participants serve as co-researchers (Stringer 2020).

This lesson introduces students to action research by allowing them to role-play as researchers and study participants in an investigation on the effects of social media. Through this activity, students will explore the social/emotional effects of social media platforms. Through role-play, students will examine issues with social media use, such as fear of missing out (FOMO), reduction in motor skills and effects on emotional well-being. The result of this pedagogical approach of role-play will be practice conducting and engaging in action research.

Through this action research project, students will role-play as researchers and participants, working together to identify the problem (e.g., social media usage), develop a plan of action to assess the specifics of the problem, collect necessary data, analyze the data, and, finally, form a conclusion. Students will then report study results to the class for peer assessment. This action research lesson can be repeated to refine results or to better understand conflicting or unexpected findings.

This role-play lesson plan is ideal for educators who want to provide students with the opportunity to practice research skills but wish to avoid common obstacles/procedures associated with conducting primary research in the field (internal review board approval, participant confidentiality, etc.). This role-play lesson will allow students to gain experience and prepare them for future research projects in various fields. Working collaboratively, teachers and students will become fully immersed in the experience of research. Through role-play, students will take on various roles to simulate aspects of formal research, such as investigating, implementing, reflecting, and refining approaches to findings. This action research role-play project also involves a reflective process that educators can use to foster student engagement and student-centered learning.

9.2 Game Details

9.2.1 Key Skills

Action research, social media, FOMO, role-play

9.2.2 Group Size

Groups of four or more – dependent on responsibilities and roles assigned applied for the research

9.2.3 Time

For this project, students will meet for a single 1-hour, 45-minute session, inclusive of role-play and debrief (times can be adjusted, or steps may be altered, to accommodate class schedules)

9.2.4 Purpose (Learning Objectives)

- Explore various applications that can help you teach, assess and provide feedback to students.
- Create a learning experience that utilizes action research and tools that can be applied in different subject areas.
- Develop a greater understanding of thoughts and actions.
- Develop understanding of teacher and student experiences.
- Provide students an opportunity to examine their experiences and generate theory.
- Develop self-awareness as practitioners, such as clarification of educational assumptions and recognition of any contradictions between ideas and actual practice.
- Practice interpreting raw data.
- Respect and value individual learning processes and experiential knowledge.
- Develop a strategy to organize data systematically strengthening the research findings and conclusions through peer-to-peer evaluation.

9.2.5 Preparation and Setup

(If technology is accessible)
Technology:

- Internet access, if students need to conduct outside research related to the project

9.2.6 Instructions

Students will engage in a role-play action research activity about the social/emotional effects of social media (e.g., Facebook, Twitter). To introduce the activity, the instructor and students should read the instructions together. The aim of the role-play study is to answer two research questions:

RQ1. What are the social/emotional effects of social media on individuals' well-being?
RQ2. How might negative effects of social media on individuals' well-being be reduced?

After reviewing the research questions, students should be divided into groups of six – if there are 24 students, there should be 4 pairs of students. For each group, assign (1) data analyst, (1) interviewer, (1) interviewee, (1) note-taker, and (1) writer. One of these students may be assigned as group leader, or all students can equally divide the leadership.

9.2.7 Data Collection Process

After all roles have been assigned, groups should begin the research to examine the social/emotional effects of social media and how those effects may be reduced. The first part of the research process will involve the group working together to develop a set of interview questions aimed at understanding the interviewees' experiences with social media, its effects on their social/emotional well-being, and ways to reduce the negative impacts of social media. Groups should brainstorm together to discuss their experiences and what kinds of questions might help them uncover data needed for the research. The group should develop a list of eight to ten questions for these purposes.

Next, the interviewer will interview the participant (interviewee), using the questions developed by the group. To avoid the need for recording or transcribing the interviews, the note-taker will listen to the interviewee's responses to the questions and take notes to capture their answers. To assist with the data recording process, the note-taker may use the observation/note-taking worksheet provided. After the interview is completed, the note-taker will provide the data analyst with the notes. The analyst will read through the notes to develop a list of themes/subthemes that seem present in the interview. The other students may join in to help the analyst with this task.

After the themes from the interviews have been developed, the data analyst will hand off the information to the writer. The writer's job is to turn the themes into a brief narrative that answers the two research questions. The writer may reference notes from the note-taker to add quotes or examples to enrich the narrative. If time permits, groups may reconvene for a second round of question development, interviews, analysis, and write-up, working with the interviewee to review the themes that were produced, discuss how improvements could be made, and then develop more finely-tuned interview questions for the second round. Iterative data collection and analysis, with the help of study participants, is a core tenet of action research.

Finally, each group will make a 5-minute presentation to share their findings with the rest of the class. The class will have the opportunity to ask questions and make comments. Groups will use those questions/comments to make revisions for final submission of their projects. At the end, the instructor will lead a class discussion on what the findings mean. Students will be encouraged to share any personal experiences/observations of the effects of social media use. The instructor should then take findings and recommendations from the groups and work with the class to develop a single list of practical recommendations for reducing the negative effects of social media use. In this way, the project not only provides students with opportunities to role-play in research but also to discuss and address some of the negative aspects of social media use.

9.2.8 Process Steps Simplified

Identify and describe the concern/research questions (10–15 minutes).
Brainstorm as a group to develop an interview protocol to address the research questions (5–10 minutes).
Collect data (30 minutes).
Analyze data and form conclusions (15–20 minutes).
Report the results and recommend a course of action (10–15 minutes).
Repeat the cycle if another session is permitted.
Discuss findings as a class.

9.2.9 Handouts and Material

Material 1: Brainstorming Worksheet/Mind Map (Exemplar)
Students should begin with a brainstorming session to develop interview questions that may help them gather data needed to answer the research questions.

Material 2: Observation/Note-Taking Worksheet (Exemplar)
Observation/note-taking worksheet will guide the note-taker in recording interview data for analysis.

Material 3: Grading Rubric
Group with the highest rating wins.

Copyright material from Hirani & Varin 2003, *Supporting Adult Learners through Games and Interactive Teaching*, Routledge

Using Role-Play to Understand Social Media 101

Material 1: Brainstorming Worksheet/Mind Map (Exemplar)

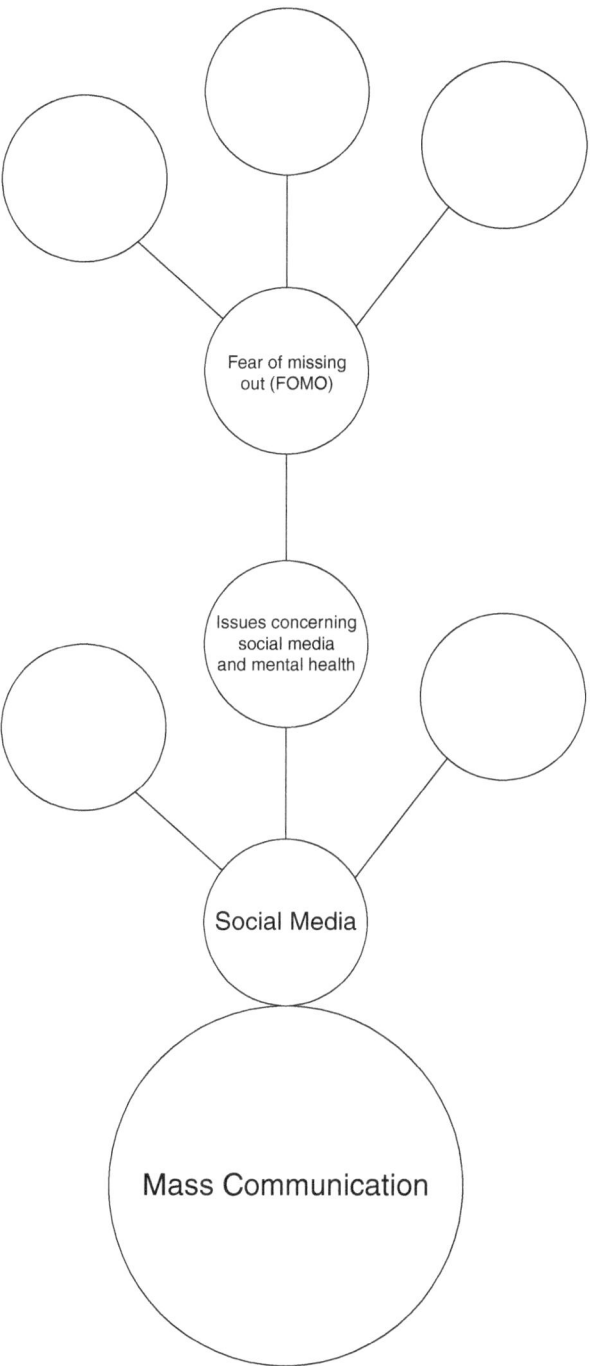

Copyright material from Hirani & Varin 2003, *Supporting Adult Learners through Games and Interactive Teaching*, Routledge

Material 2: Observation/Note-Taking Worksheet (Exemplar)

Role-Play Observation Journal
Group Name(s):
Date(s):

(This is for example purposes only. Students may explore other options to write their journals.)

Directions:

Use this worksheet to capture interviewees' responses to each of the interview questions asked. When you can, try to capture direct quotes that may be really relevant. In addition, take notes on the interviewee's body language and physical cues. For example, if the interviewee hesitates to answer a question, looks around, seems particularly emotional (e.g., happy, sad, excited), shifts their body, or uses hand gestures, make a note of it. Fill out the Table 9.1 with each of the interview questions. For each question's corresponding rows and columns, record interviewee responses and your observations.

Table 9.1 Observation/Note-Taking Worksheet

Interview Question	Notes on Responses	Observations
1.		
2.		
3.		
4.		
5.		
6.		
7.		
8.		

Material 3: Grading Rubric (Rubric can be modified based on instructional needs)

Copyright material from Hirani & Varin 2003, *Supporting Adult Learners through Games and Interactive Teaching*, Routledge

Table 9.2 Grading Rubric

Area	Rating	Comments
Quality of information provided (e.g., presentation main points are clear and well developed, information is linked to the topic, well organized discussion)		
Data analysis (e.g., the data shows deep insight into the dataset by drawing specific conclusions that require careful or multi-level analysis of the data. Results may be particularly surprising or interesting)		
Theme development (e.g., shows a thorough and thoughtful understanding of the text, the group demonstrates understanding of the key concepts or issues important to the topic and can answer questions from the class)		
Presentation skills (e.g., appropriate use of terminology, terms applied to the language required to describe the content, terms were used in creative ways to help the audience understand)		

Group Name(s):

Directions – Utilize the following rubric for the groups to peer evaluate the quality of information provided, data analysis, theme development, and presentation skills. The scoring rubric communicates expectations of the role-play activity. Rate each of the following areas as excellent (3), good (2) or needs work (1). Add comments to explain your rating and answer the questions in Table 9.2.

9.3 Adaptation of the Games to a Different Context

Role-plays to demonstrate action research in various settings are simple to set up. The following examples demonstrate various applications that can help you teach, assess, and provide feedback for your students.

1. **Fake News?** The goal of this project is to explore media literacy and critical thinking skills. Students may develop their own research questions on the topic, with the objective of figuring out ways to use critical thinking to discern media messages.

Copyright material from Hirani & Varin 2003, *Supporting Adult Learners through Games and Interactive Teaching*, Routledge

2. **Healthy Eating.** The role-play action project can also be applied to examine healthy eating patterns and nutrition decisions. Students may develop questions aimed at understanding how we establish diet patterns, why unhealthy nutritional decisions are made, and what they can do to eat in a way that provides better nourishment to their bodies.
3. **How Do You Learn?** For this topic, students may explore the different styles of learning (visual/spatial, aural, verbal, physical, logical, social, and solitary). The goal is to understand the learning style of the interviewee and develop a list of recommendations to help that interviewee improve their learning. Through this activity, students will have the opportunity to reflect on their own learning styles and ways they can improve their learning through specific strategies.

The point of these activities is to put learning into the student's hands – it's about them, not us! By creating an environment of discovery, students will not rely on the teacher as the sole source of information. This abbreviated version of action research through this role-play activity can be applied to explore, discover and create their own way to interpret information.

Notes

1 FOMO or the "fear of missing out" is a feeling of worry that an interesting or exciting event is happening somewhere else." FOMO (n.d.). Oxford. Retrieved 3 June 2021, from https://www.oxfordlearnersdictionaries.com/us/definition/english/fomo?q=fear+of+missing+out.
2 Social Media refers to websites and software programs used for social networking. Social media (n.d.). Oxford. Retrieved 3 June 2021, from https://www.oxfordlearnersdictionaries.com/us/definition/english/social-media?q=social+media.

Bibliography

Gardner, H. (2011). *Frames of mind: The theory of multiple intelligences*. New York: Basic Books.

Latif, R., Mumtaz, S., Mumtaz, R., and Hussain, A. (2018). A comparison of debate and Role-play in enhancing critical thinking and communication skills of medical students during problem based learning. *Biochemistry and Molecular Biology Education*, 46(4), pp. 336–42. https://doi.org/10.1002/bmb.21124

Lewin, K. (1946). Action research and minority problems. *Journal of Social Issues*, 2(4), pp. 34–46. https://doi.org/10.1111/j.1540-4560.1946.tb02295.x

McCarthy, J. P., and Anderson, L. (1999). Active learning techniques versus traditional teaching styles: Two experiments from history and political science. *Innovative Higher Education*, 24(4), pp. 279–94. https://doi.org/10.1023/b:ihie.0000047415.48495.05

Minhas, P. S., Ghosh, A., and Swanzy, L. (2012). The effects of passive and active learning on student preference and performance in an undergraduate basic science course. *Anatomical Sciences Education*, 5(4), pp. 200–7. https://doi.org/10.1002/ase.1274

Planander, U. W. A. (2013). Role-play as a pedagogical method to prepare students for practice: The students' voice. *Högre Utbildning*, 3(3), pp. 199–210. http://www.hogreutbildning.se

Prince, M. (2004). Does active learning work? A review of the research. *Journal of Engineering Education*, 93(3), pp. 223–31. https://doi.org/10.1002/j.2168-9830.2004.tb00809.x

Rahman, N. A., & Maarof, N. (2018). The effect of role-play and simulation approach on enhancing ESL oral communication skills. *International Journal of Research in English Education*, 3(3), pp. 64–71. http://ijreeonline.com/

Rao, D., & Stupans, I. (2012). Exploring the potential of Role-play in higher education: Development of a typology and teacher guidelines. *Innovations in Education and Teaching International*, 49(4), pp. 427–36. https://doi.org/10.1080/14703297.2012.728879

Ruhanen, L. (2005). Bridging the divide between theory and practice. *Journal of Teaching in Travel & Tourism*, 5(4), pp. 33–51. https://doi.org/10.1300/j172v05n04_03

Shapiro, S., & Leopold, L. (2012). A critical role for role-playing pedagogy. *TESL Canada Journal*, 29(2), pp. 120. https://doi.org/10.18806/tesl.v29i2.1104

Stringer, E. T. (2020). *Action research*. Thousand Oaks, CA: SAGE Publications.

10 Games on a Grid (I)
Noughts and Crosses

Philippa Mullins

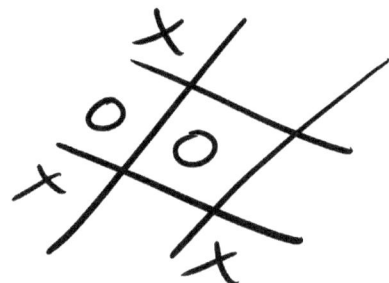

10.1 Overview

A simple playground-style grid laid out on the ground creates opportunities to practice team-building and cooperation, problem-solving, and making and defending an argument in response to an opposing team, while also revising material that has been previously introduced in class.

Applicable to any material covered in class, this game also allows the facilitator to reframe learning more generally. Both students and teachers often demonstrate resistance to active, game-based learning. One explanation for this is that, while students in fact learn more through active approaches, they perceive that they are learning less due to the increased effort which active learning requires (Deslauriers et al. 2019). Deslauriers et al. suggest that this misperception should be tackled directly to improve student engagement in active learning. Challenging exclusionary oppositions between 'fun' and 'serious learning', I suggest that playing and reflecting on this game of noughts and crosses also provides a direct pathway to discussing how active participation and play can improve learning more widely.

So, what is the game? At its simplest, noughts and crosses (or tic tac toe) is played by two teams of students who must answer questions in order to place a team member on the large grid, which is marked out on the ground. The winner is the first team to place three team members in a straight line. Beginning from a simple version, noughts and crosses can subsequently be extended to ensure that students remain challenged and to guide learning in

DOI: 10.4324/9781003230120-10

different areas. Adjusting who writes the questions, how the group decides whether or not a question has been answered in a way that permits a player to step onto the grid, whether and how answers are recorded, and how the answers are used next are just some ways to develop the game. I encourage you also to invent your own extensions and adaptations as you play.

Before moving to the game, a note on the importance of encouraging a playful attitude to it. Nørgård, Claus, and Whitton argue that a risk with games is that they in fact "focus primarily on outcomes, competition, and extrinsic rewards, and thus, in effect, [echo] the performative culture of the [university] sector" (2017, 273). They describe games as potentially developing extrinsic motivation, decreasing intrinsic motivation, and promoting a tendency to manipulate a system for points (ibid., 273; cf. also: Baker et al. 2008; Deci et al. 2001). In proposing a game which allows 'moves' to be made based on a right answer being given, I am highly aware of the need for facilitators to set a playful spirit which does not promote the replication of a single restricted answer to gain points.

How this is approached depends on the material being revised. However, in all cases, original phrasing should be encouraged, as opposed to the production of a single definition. Facilitators should encourage definitions and concepts to be illustrated by students' own examples, and attempts to bring together disparate material in a new way should be praised and rewarded. The aim here is to focus on the ideas brought out through the process of playing, rather than foregrounding a binary 'win-lose' outcome. This can also be encouraged in how the game is played. For example, teams can be regularly mixed and switched between rounds. Original answers and striking examples should be highlighted in reflection following the game, independent of which team they came from.

The remainder of this chapter is structured as follows. Firstly, I outline how the game is played, offering instructions, troubleshooting guidance, and one framework for how to debrief. Secondly, I present several extensions to the game. Here, for example, debate elements can be added, and students can use their answers to develop mind maps and essay plans. I encourage the facilitator to trial their own extensions and adjustments, and to work out extensions and adjustments together with the group. Using imagination to develop the game and negotiating such adjustments as a group are transferable skills in themselves.

10.2 Games Details

10.2.1 Key Skills

Communication, cooperation, problem-solving, building an argument through dialogue

10.2.2 Group Size

Each game is played by two teams of four-five people, in an overall group of eight-ten.

For example, a class of 30 people could be divided into three overall groups of ten. Within these overall groups of ten, two teams of four people would play against each other and two people from the overall group would be left to ask questions and run the game (see p. 000).

The game is fairly adaptable to the size of the group. For adaptations using larger teams (e.g., six-seven people), see Section 10.3.

10.2.3 Time

The activity generally needs around 45 minutes to an hour, particularly the first time it is played. Afterwards, it is possible to play quick-fire versions taking around 20–30 minutes.

10.2.4 Purpose (Learning Objectives)

1. To review previously learnt material in a fun way
2. To develop communication skills between team members as they negotiate a strategy around where on the grid to place players
3. To develop communication and presentation skills as team members answer questions orally to win their place on the grid
4. To develop skills at critically evaluating others' arguments, as one team may challenge the opposing team's answer to prevent them from winning a place on the grid

10.2.5 Preparation and Setup

10.2.5.1 Materials Needed

- Something to mark a grid on the floor, e.g., either masking tape or chalk to outline the grid or pieces of paper where each one forms a place on the grid
- Question cards

10.2.5.2 Preparing the Question Cards

- Questions can be written out on small pieces of paper.
- They should reflect the material that has been covered in the course.
- They may be written by the course leader or by students.
- To facilitate the students writing the question cards, you could use an 'exit ticket' system at the end of each or some classes:
  - At the end of the class, dedicate 5 minutes for students to write down a question on a piece of card.
  - One prompt could be, "Write down a question you have learnt the answer to in the course so far."
    - E.g., What is one definition of [*concept*]?

- E.g., What are two critiques of [*concept*]?
    - E.g., When does [*X*] cause [*Y*]? When does it not?
- Another prompt could be, "What questions do you still have about the subject we have been talking about today?"
    - E.g., What does [*term*] mean?
    - E.g., How does [*process*] work?
    - E.g., What are two suggestions for improving [*situation*]?
- Model examples from your course material will support students to do this.
- Student-written question cards may then need to be checked and curated by the course leader and/or by peers before they are included in the pack of question cards for the game.
- If there is not enough open space for the physical version of the game, a table-top version may be played by using paper and pens (see Section 10.3).

10.2.6 Instructions

Mark out the grid on the floor.
You can use chalk or masking tape or string and tape to mark out the lines.
Otherwise, you could mark out each of the squares with pieces of paper or card.
Anything to make a grid that everyone can follow.

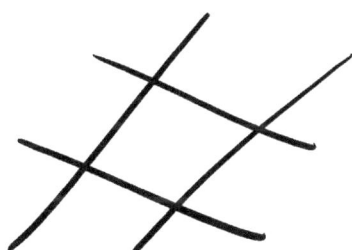

Figure 10.1 Grid markings.

Divide into teams.
Teams can be of three to four people. Make sure to leave people to be Question Masters, if needed. For adaptations with bigger teams, see Section 10.3.

Decide on the Question Masters.
Maybe the facilitator is the Question Master, or maybe it is other students. Have one to two Question Masters for each game.

110 *Philippa Mullins*

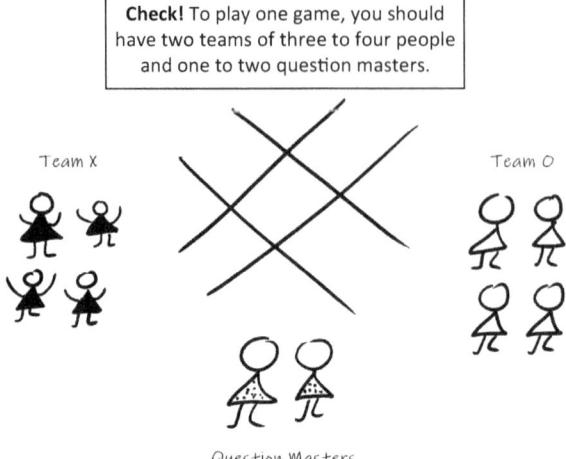

Figure 10.2 Player setup around the grid.

The Question Masters pick a question from the pack.

They ask the question to one team.

That team answers the question.

If the team gets the answer correct, they may place a player on the grid.
Generally, the Question Masters decide whether the answer is enough to place a player on the grid; see the "Guidance" section for further information on this.

Figure 10.3 Players moving into the grid.

Next, the Question Masters ask a different question to the other team, who must also answer correctly to place a player on the grid.

The game continues alternating between teams.

The winning team is the team which places three players in a straight line on the board first.

After you have finished playing, move to the debrief (see p. 000).

Figure 10.4 Winning team formation in the grid.

10.2.7 Guidance

The game itself is fairly simple. However, there are a few aspects that need further attention to ensure everything goes smoothly.

How to introduce the game to the group?
You could play one round game with 'fun questions' so that the group first becomes comfortable with how it works. For example, the facilitator could ask teams questions like, "How many people in the room are wearing the colour green?", or "Guess what winter month I am born in!", or even "3+4=?"
Adapt the questions to the group. This mode of using the game acts both as a warm-up and to get everyone acquainted with how it works.
If group members have not played the game before at all, it may be helpful to play a round on the board as an example, before then playing it with 'fun questions' and finally playing it with revision questions from the course.
To demonstrate the game on the board, the facilitator should draw the grid and make the first move and then invite someone from the class to make the next move as a representative of the opposing team. The game then alternates between the facilitator and a different group member until it is over. Either the facilitator can pick a different group member each time, or the group member should nominate the next group member to play.

Which team goes first?
In this game, it is an advantage to go first. If you are playing one round only, the Question Masters should decide randomly which team plays first. If you are playing more rounds after that, the teams should alternate.
The Question Master(s) can decide randomly who goes first by:

- *Spinning a pen or a pencil. The team towards which the writing end of the pen or pencil points most plays first.*
- *Writing down a number between one and five on a piece of paper without showing it to either team. Ask the teams to each guess a number between one and five. Whichever team is closest to the number the Question Master wrote down plays first.*

Is it over after one game?
The game can be played as a one-off, or as a 'best of three rounds' (i.e., you play the game three times, and the team with the most victories win), or for any other number of rounds. If the teams end up tied on the same score, either leave it there or play a tie-break game to decide the winner.

How much time do players have to answer a question?
This may depend on the nature of the question, how comfortable and confident the players are, and on whether conferring is allowed. However, as a rule, players should not have too long to answer; once they are used to the game, 1 or 2 minutes should be enough. The Question Masters can time this, or just push the team for an answer, if they feel too much time has passed.

Who answers the questions?
There are different versions of this. You could decide that the whole team may confer and answer the question together. Then you would also have to decide if more than one person may speak to communicate the answer to the wider group, or if only the person who is to step onto the grid, if the answer is right, may speak.
Otherwise, the team should nominate a player to answer the question alone. That player would then step onto the grid if their answer is correct.
In the latter case, you may set the rule that the player who has to answer the question must be nominated by their team either before or after the question has been read out. This depends on how difficult you want to make the game; setting the nomination of the player to answer the question alone before the question has been heard means that the team cannot strategically choose a player who feels more comfortable with an already-known question.
Once players are on the grid, they may not help answer questions.
Answering as a team may be more effective to work on within-group communication under time pressure. Answering as an individual builds comfort with presentation skills, as individuals have to speak in front of the whole group.

When is an answer 'enough' to get to place a player on the grid?
The Question Masters should decide whether an answer is sufficient to allow the team to place their player on the grid. The facilitator may need to work together with the Question Master(s) to support this decision. In an extension of the game, answers may also be challenged by the opposing team (see Section 10.3). Depending on the nature of the material being revised, this can also be a chance to disrupt any preconceived ideas around any single 'correct' answer. The facilitator may lead discussion in the debrief around how multiple answers may be 'correct' and re-emphasise the importance of presenting an evidenced argument for whatever answer is being put forward.

10.2.8 Debrief

The following questions should help the participants to reflect on the game. They will also help the facilitators to understand participants' experiences and learning. It may not be necessary to ask all questions each time. The facilitator can change how the debrief is done depending on time remaining, participants' energy levels, and how much or little the game has been played (as some questions may become less relevant).

10.2.9 Learning and the Course

As well as structuring self-reflection for participants on their learning and the course material, these questions will help update the question pack.

> *What is one question you now feel more confident about?*
> *What is one question you still have after the session?*
> *What is one question you think is important and which you were not asked today?*

As students reflect on these questions, the facilitator can draw out reflection on how they perceive their learning. Given that active learning may feel harder because of the effort it demands (Deslauriers et al. 2019), it is valuable to question perceptions of effort and progress. Recording these reflections over time can also produce a record allowing students to look further back to identify change and achievement. This is particularly the case where progress may be so incremental as to make it harder to identify after one or two sessions.

Structuring discussions around change and achievement through the game can also challenge the assumption that, if playing a game, you are not really learning. On the other hand, discussing effort, confusion and discomfort can build students' comfort with being uncomfortable. Here the facilitator can frame being uncomfortable as a natural, necessary and positive part of learning. All these discussions may help to normalise the idea of using games and an active learning style more generally in whatever course you are teaching.

Framing questions can include:

> *How did you feel about the game?*
> *What do you think you are learning?*
> *Why might it feel difficult?*
> *What does something 'feeling difficult' mean?*

10.2.10 Working with My Team

These questions will help to lead discussion about participants' experiences of the game, as well as about teamwork and other skills practiced.

> *How were decisions made in my team?*
> *Did we hear everyone's voices when we conferred?*
> *How did I feel when I had to present my answer?*
> *How did I feel when I was challenged?*

The questions may be presented in different ways. They may be answered first by individuals, potentially making 'exit ticket'–style notes, which you then collect up. After individual reflection, with or without notes, you could move into group reflection. You could then pair groups to share reflections more widely and fix them in a mind map or illustration. Alternatively, you could then have groups report back to the whole class and have a few participants capture what was said by writing on the board.

10.3 Adaptation of the Games to a Different Context

The game can be extended in the following ways:

10.3.1 Table-Top Version

If there is no room to mark out any grid on the floor, the game may be played on a piece of paper. The same rules are used, but rather than playing by physically putting a player in a space, the team will just draw their sign on a big grid made on a piece of paper.

10.3.2 Team Size

With a bigger group, you can adapt the game to play 'connect four' or 'connect five'. The grid becomes bigger and to win teams must connect four or five players in a straight line (horizontal, vertical, or diagonal).

- **Challenge Cards**
  Each team may have a number of challenge cards they can use (two cards for noughts and crosses, three cards for 'connect four', etc.). They may play these cards to challenge a decision made by the Question Master. For example:

  - The Question Master asks Team O a question.
  - Team O answers.
  - The Question Master approves the answer.
  - The Question Master then asks Team X if they want to challenge the decision. They have limited time to decide and formulate their challenge. The facilitator may amend the time depending on the group and the type of question.
  - If Team X does not decide to challenge, Team O may place a player on the grid.

- If Team X decides to challenge, it must surrender a challenge card to the Question Master and make its point about a weakness in Team O's answer.
- Team O then may respond.
- If the response is not satisfactory, Team O may not place a player on the grid. Team X gets its challenge card back.
- If the response is satisfactory, Team O may place a player. Team X does not get its challenge card back.
- It is generally the Question Master who decides. The facilitator may support. Discussion should be open, weighing up the different points of the argument.

- **Thematic Versions**
  Questions can be general, covering an entire course. Alternatively, they can look more in-depth at a particular argument or part of the course. In this case, there can be many questions around the same topic aiming at building more depth of knowledge. This is particularly useful for working with extensions of the game: Scribes and mind maps.
- **Scribes and Mind Maps**
  You can have one or two people on the team noting down both teams' answers in a single game. Alternatively, you can have someone who is a Scribe for each game (as with Question Masters, make sure Scribes rotate so that everyone tries out all the roles in the end). Get Scribes to note down answers on a grid mirroring the one on which the game is played.

  After the game, this will leave you with a grid full of answers. Mix up the teams, and run a follow-on activity where teams cut up the grid and stick the answers on a bigger sheet either as:

  - A **mind map**: add to the answers and make connections between them.
  - An **essay plan**: try to rearrange the points into a structured argument. Add to them and edit them where needed. The facilitator may give an organising question. Alternatively, participants may try to work one out themselves.

Bibliography

Baker, R., J. Walonoski, N. Heffernan, I. Roll, A. Corbett, and K. Koedinger. (2008). Why students engage in 'gaming the system' behavior in interactive learning environments. *Journal of Interactive Learning Research*, 19(2), pp. 162–82.

Deci, Edward L., Richard Koestner, and Richard M. Ryan. (2001). Extrinsic rewards and intrinsic motivation in education: reconsidered once again. *Review of Educational Research*, 71(1), pp. 1–27.

Deslauriers, Louis, Logan S. McCarty, Kelly Miller, Kristina Callaghan, and Greg Kestin. (2019). Measuring actual learning versus feeling of learning in response to being actively engaged in the classroom. *Proceedings of the National Academy of Sciences*, 116(39), pp. 19251–57.

Nørgård, Rikke Toft, Claus Toft-Nielsen, and Nicola Whitton. (2017). Playful learning in higher education: developing a signature pedagogy. *International Journal of Play*, 6(3), pp. 272–82.

11 Games on a Grid (II)

Hotspot

Rachel Warnick

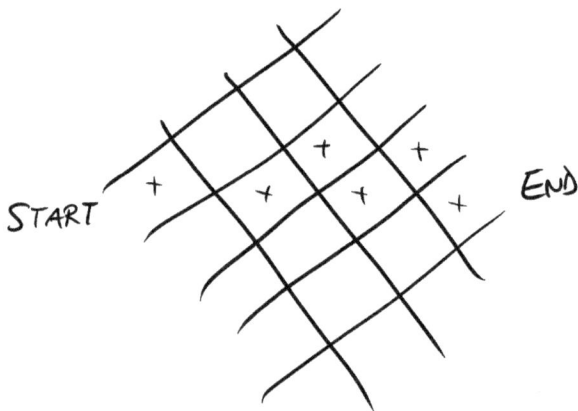

11.1 Overview

This activity is not specific to any subject and thus can easily be used by any facilitator to supplement skills learning amongst their students. The skills taught in this activity are essential to academic and professional success, and as such, they will serve the students in any subject, discipline or career.

Learning through games can provide a form of experiential learning. According to David Kolb's theory, this offers "the process whereby knowledge is created through the transformation of experience. Knowledge results from the combinations of grasping and transforming the experience" (Kolb 1984). Participants learn, not only by actively doing but by *reflecting* on their experiences in order to be able to apply their learning across multiple contexts.

As noted in the chapter titled "Games on a Grid (I): Noughts and Crosses", there can often be resistance to game-based learning, as the element of fun may appear to negate its deeper benefits. This could be considered a valid argument if the metacognitive debriefing component is excluded. It is the post-activity reflection that is crucial for participants to successfully find and construct meaning in the experience and to retain that knowledge in the long term.

DOI: 10.4324/9781003230120-11

For educators that are not accustomed to leading reflective debriefing sessions, these can initially seem daunting, but this chapter provides a wide range of questions that can be applied to a multitude of activities, subjects and contexts outside this particular game as well. Through time and experience, guiding students through debriefing sessions becomes easier, more effective and more enjoyable.

Hotspot is an excellent example of, and simple entry into, game-based learning. In this problem-solving game, a group of students must work as a team to navigate through the grid from the entry to exit points while avoiding the hidden 'hotspots'. The facilitator designs a grid and marks a 'safe' route between the entry and exit squares. The remaining squares are hotspots that students must avoid (the number and layout of these determine the level of difficulty). Once the grid is mapped out on the ground, students take turns navigating the correct route through it by stepping on squares one at a time. If the student steps onto a hotspot square, the facilitator will ask them to leave the grid and the next student starts their turn. The game is finished when a student successfully navigates the entire grid from entry to exit in one turn. With large groups of students, this game can be played by multiple teams racing against each other to finish first. This game also provides an opportunity to work on observation, reasoning and deductive skills. Playing a version that permits talking can help develop teamwork skills, while playing a silent version can also help flex non-verbal communication skills. In addition, debriefing can examine the issues of leadership and decision-making.

The activity is intentionally designed to have minimal warm-up and introduction to ensure that the participants feel the discomfort of uncertainty and react to working with little information. This activity can be run in a workshop for educators to give them the experience and understanding of how the debriefing process works and the value it offers participants to process and deepen their learning.

11.2 Games Details

11.2.1. Key Skills

Communication, teamwork, leadership, problem-solving, failing forward (learning through mistakes)

11.2.2 Group Size

This activity works best with groups of four to eight students. For larger groups, subdivide into groups of four to eight and run them concurrently.

11.2.3 Time

The length of this activity will depend on your group and the size of your grid. A 5×5 grid, for example, can take 10–30 minutes.

11.2.4 Purpose (Learning Objectives)

1. To demonstrate the value of failing forward (learning through mistakes)
2. To illustrate the necessity of working together as a team
3. To improve communication skills (verbal or non-verbal)
4. To practice problem-solving through an activity requiring deductive reasoning
5. To examine how leadership is assumed, accepted and manifested

11.2.5 Preparation and Setup

Room –

- The room should be large enough to mark out a grid of the selected size on the floor with sufficient space for one person to comfortably stand on two feet inside a square without touching the demarcating lines.
- The recommended grid size limits are 5 × 5 squares minimum (normally the ideal size) and 8 × 8 squares maximum.
- There also needs to be enough space surrounding the grid for every person in the group to fully view the action, especially the facilitator.
- Materials commonly used to demarcate the grid include chalk or masking tape (not translucent tape). If these are not available, a tile floor provides an obvious grid by using common classroom objects, such as books to mark off the four external corners.
- Surfaces that retain visible footprints, such as dirt floors, will make the activity too easy and participants will not fully benefit from the challenges and learning benefits.

Technology –

- No technology is required for this activity.
- However, if you have a smartphone with a sound effects app such as Sound Effects or Pow Soundbox (both of which are free), this can add an element of fun (or pressure!) to the activity (Figures 11.1 to 11.4).

11.2.6 Guidance

Be sure to have a copy of your planned route through the grid with you while running the activity, as it can be difficult to remember during the action.

Be aware that the route may be visible through the paper as you hold it up and take any necessary precautions to conceal it, such as putting an additional paper or a book behind it.

If you are using chalk to demarcate your grid, try to prevent the participants from treading on the lines so that they are not blurred or erased as the activity progresses.

Depending on where you position yourself, it may be helpful to turn your route map to correspond with your view of the grid. For example, if you are standing at the 'top' near the exit square, then you might wish to turn the map 'upside down' to match your view. This can help prevent errors in switching between looking at the map and looking at the real floor grid because you are seeing both from the same perspective.

Games on a Grid (II) 119

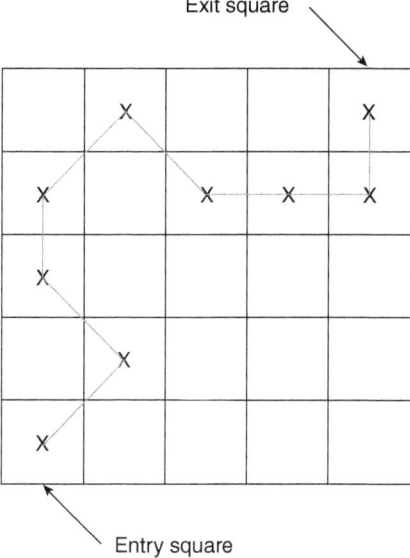

Figure 11.1 Example route (simple).

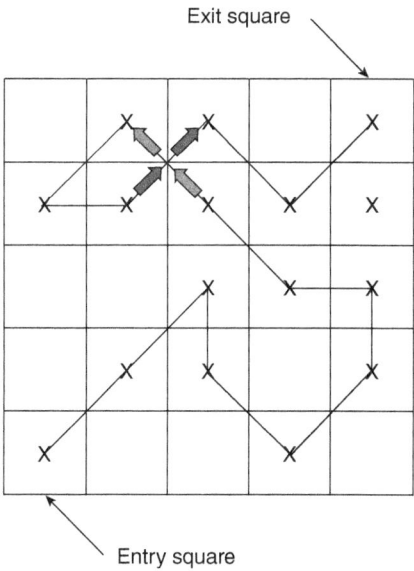

Figure 11.2 Example route (complex).

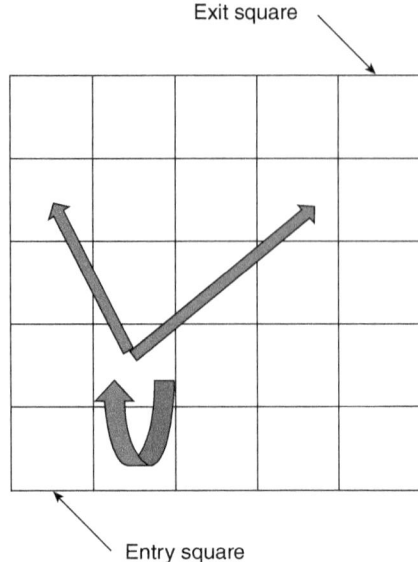

Figure 11.3 Forbidden moves.

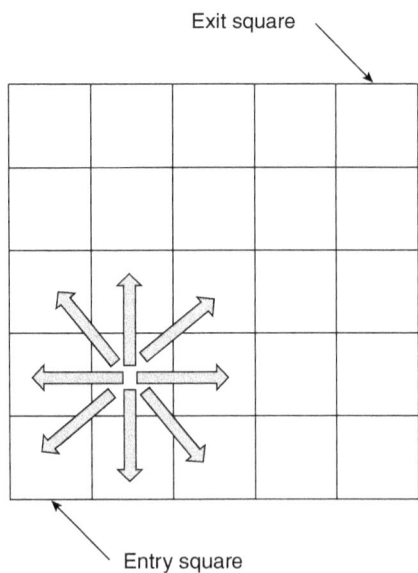

Figure 11.4 Permitted moves.

Numbering the participants can be useful to help them remember the order and to monitor full participation.

It is recommended to select only a single noise for incorrect moves and remain consistent with it throughout the activity.

If you are using a sound effects app, lengthen or disable your phone's screen time-out setting while conducting the activity; otherwise, it can cause a delay in your response time to incorrect guesses and a drag in the activity (and therefore, reduce engagement).

If you are running the activity with a single group, you may choose to place a time limit on selecting the next move if you want to further increase the pressure of the challenge. A limit of 15–20 seconds would be reasonable for this purpose. A time limit of 60 seconds could be useful to keep the activity moving (and engagement high) if you know your participants have high potential to become mired in cautious deliberations. However, time limits are not a necessary component of the activity, and it normally works equally well without them.

If you are running the activity for two groups at the same time, adding a competitive element makes it more exciting and engaging by naturally increasing the pressure. Time limits are not recommended in such cases.

When running the activity for two groups at the same time, you will need an additional person to monitor the second grid and this person will require a copy of the correct route and a thorough understanding of the rules.

If you are running the activity for two groups at the same time, you may choose to have a different route for each group (Route A and Route B) so that they do not learn from each other. However, if you plan to run it a second time after mixing up the groups, it is recommended to use Route A for both groups on the first attempt and Route B for both groups on the second attempt, so as not to unnecessarily complicate facilitation. In this case, you should place them far enough apart to prevent 'copying', if you have sufficient space.

If you run the activity a second time after mixing up the groups, it is most likely that it will take considerably less time.

In the event that a group asks for time to strategise or plan before starting, it is at the discretion of the facilitator whether or not to permit this. However, it is not recommended to offer this when no request has been made by the participants, as it provides a valuable line of questioning when debriefing the activity, particularly if the learning objectives are problem-solving or failing forward (learning through mistakes).

11.2.7 Instructions

11.2.7.1 Preparation

In the planning stage, draw a grid on paper and decide what route you wish the participants to take from the entry square to the exit square (normally bottom left to top right or vice versa).

The route should include at least a few twists and turns (Figure 11.1). The more of these you include, the greater the challenge for the participants (Figure 11.2).

The route must not require the participants to pass through the same square twice (Figure 11.3).

The route must pass from one square directly to another adjacent square in any direction (horizontal, vertical or diagonal; Figure 11.4) and should not require a jump to another square that is not in direct contact (Figure 11.3).

The route must not be revealed to the participants prior to or during the activity.

Decide the relevant narrative for your context (quicksand, minefield, bridge over water, et cetera).

Decide which noise you will use to indicate that a participant has stepped on an incorrect square. This could be a sound relevant to your context (for example, a splash for a bridge over water, an explosion for a minefield, a sucking or slurping noise for quicksand) or simply a loud and amusing sound effect (such as a crowing rooster, a braying donkey, the crack of a whip, an exaggerated exclamation like "WAAAH!" or "YIKES!" or "OUCH!") to inject humour and increase engagement.

Decide whether you wish to allow the participants to communicate verbally, if they can make non-verbal noises such as clapping, snapping or stomping or if they must remain completely silent throughout the activity.

11.2.7.2 Setup

Mark out the grid on the floor using the method relevant to your materials.

If you are using a sound effects app, have your sound effect ready to play.

Divide the participants into sub-groups if working with groups larger than approximately eight people.

Assign or have the participants determine the order in which they will take their turns.

11.2.7.3 Instructions

Instruct the participants that they must find the invisible route from the entry square to the exit square. Ensure the participants know which squares these are.

Inform them that there is only one correct route through the grid and that you hold the solution in your hand.

Participants will take turns one at a time in passing through the grid and attempting to find the correct route.

Participants can only move one square in any direction (horizontally, vertically or diagonally) to an adjacent square. Jumping squares is not permitted.

Stepping on any squares that are not on the correct route will result in the end of the participant's turn (falling into quicksand/stepping on a landmine/falling off the bridge).

Inform the participants that you will alert them to an incorrect choice by making a noise, and then demonstrate that noise. Advise them that you will not make any noise when they make a correct choice.

Once any part of a participant's foot touches the floor in the next square selected, the participant cannot change his/her/their mind, regardless of how light or brief the touch was.

At the end of a participant's turn, he/she/they must leave the grid, and the next participant starts his/her/their turn.

Every participant on every turn always begins their turn at the entry square. Participants are not allowed to return directly to the last correct square. They must walk the entire correct route from entry to exit.

If you have decided to run this as a non-verbal or silent activity, inform the participants that no talking or vocal sound of any kind is permitted from this moment until completion and whether or not they are allowed to make any non-verbal noises.

11.2.7.4 Facilitation

Advise the group that they may begin.
The first participant steps into the entry square.
The participant then selects which adjacent square to step into next.
If the square selected is correct, do nothing and allow the same participant to proceed with his/her/their next selection.
If the square selected is incorrect (that is, not on the route you have mapped out), inform the group by making your chosen noise.
Ensure that the participant leaves the grid and the next participant begins their turn on the entry square.
Allow the activity to proceed in this manner until one student traces the entire route correctly from the entry square to the exit square without a single error.

11.2.8 Debrief

The facilitator may select from the following list of questions according to the learning objectives he/she/they wish to highlight. Not all questions within each group need to be covered, and the facilitator is welcome to pick and choose the questions that are most relevant to the group and the context.

There are several options for gathering responses to these questions, and these can be combined:

- Call on individual participants to answer orally and generate a class discussion.
- Subdivide the class into smaller groups of three to five people. Provide the questions to the groups (in written form or on a chalkboard/whiteboard) and have each group discuss them internally before sharing with the entire group.
- If two teams competed by playing concurrently in competition, the facilitator could:
  - Provide the questions to the groups (in written form or on a chalkboard/whiteboard) and have each group discuss them internally before sharing with the entire group.
  - Mix the groups so that participants from both teams are in each group. Then provide the questions to the groups (in written form or on a chalkboard/whiteboard) and have each group discuss them internally. The facilitator can choose whether to circulate among the groups to monitor the discussions or have the groups share highlights of their discussions with the entire group.

- Ask participants to prepare a written response to questions. This can be done during class or as homework. It is recommended that only a few questions are assigned in this manner and that the more reflective ones – that is, questions on how the lessons learned from the activity connect with real-life situations – are selected for this method.

11.2.8.1. General

What were your expectations at the beginning of the activity?
What did you think or feel while doing the activity?
What were your greatest successes or frustrations?

11.2.8.2. Problem-Solving

How many different strategies did your team try or use?
What made you decide to adapt or change your strategies?
Did your team plan or strategise before starting the activity? Why or why not? (These questions do not apply if it was run as a non-verbal or silent activity.)
Would it have made any difference if you had devised a strategy prior to starting? Explain your answer.
What did you learn about problem-solving from this activity, and how can this be applied to other areas of your life?

11.2.8.3. Failing Forward

Each time you failed, how did you feel? Why?
Did every failure feel the same? Why or why not?
What did you do to tackle any negative feelings you experienced from your failures?
Is failure always negative? Why or why not?
What did you learn about failure from this activity, and how can this be applied to other areas of your life?

11.2.8.4. Communications

How well did your team communicate? Give reasons and examples to support your answer.
How did you communicate your ideas? (This question is especially important if it was run as a non-verbal or silent activity.)
Did everyone feel heard? Why or why not?
When conflicting ideas arose, how did the group decide which idea was best?
What would have been the best way to communicate during this activity? How can this be applied to other contexts in your life?

11.2.8.5. Teamwork

Did you work well as a group? Why or why not?

How did the group reach agreement and take group decisions? Why do you think it happened this way?

Did the whole team agree on the decisions that were made?

- *If not, was this resolved? If yes, how was that achieved? If not, what effect did that have on the group?*
- *If so, how was that achieved?*

Was there anything that one of the group members did that was particularly helpful? What was it and why?

In what way did you support your group members?

What support did you get from your group? What difference did this make to you and why?

Did any member of the group feel left out? Why or why not?

Was there any negativity in the group at any time?

- *If so, what effect did it have on the group, and how was it managed?*
- *If not, what do you think that was?*

What do you think is the most important element of teamwork? How can this be applied to other activities and contexts in your life?

11.2.8.6. Leadership

Did anyone emerge as a leader during this activity?

- *If so, who was it, and why do you think that was? Do you think you would have performed better with a different leader? Without a leader? Why or why not?*
- *If not, why do you think that was? How did the group manage without a leader? Do you think you would have performed better if you had had one? Why or why not?*

Did the leadership shift or change during the activity? If so, how and why?

If a leader emerged:

- *Was he/she/they a good leader? Why or why not?*
- *How did the leader manage the group?*
- *How did the leader communicate?*
- *What could the leader have done better?*

What are the qualities or skills a leader needs to have? What is his/her/their purpose?

Is the leader responsible for the success or failure of the group? Why or why not?

11.2.9 Handouts and Material

No handouts are required for this activity.

Bibliography

Kolb, D. A. (1984). *Experiential learning: experience as the source of learning and development.* Hoboken, New Jersey: Prentice-Hall.

12 A Fantasy Game to Illustrate the Psychology of Power and Information Asymmetry

Rudi Ackerman

12.1 Overview

Originally designed as part of a psychology class in Soviet Russia by Dimitry Davidoff in 1986, *Mafia* is a social deduction group game that illustrates the power and psychology of information asymmetry. The game later became a popular party game in many parts of the world, and several variants have since been developed. This chapter uses the popular *Werewolf* variant as a learning tool in a class setting.

The game's central premise is that an informed minority is pitted against an uninformed majority. In many cases, the minority ends up winning because of rampant mistrust and a lack of cohesive action from the majority. The emotive way that players are eliminated from the game gives it great heuristic value because students deeply experience each decision they make in the game. The game has been extensively used in high school and university classrooms, and its dynamics are well studied.[1]

In the real world, many of the games we play divide us between various minority and majority groups with asymmetric access to information. We might be in a group of 'factory workers' who do not have much power over budgeting decisions for our company. By contrast, we might be in the 'executives' group that wields immense power over decisions around who stays and who leaves. This form of information asymmetry and power imbalance is perceived as fair within the social construction of most corporations today. However, alternative formations of group organisation do exist, from traditional Masaai land usage rights decided by a collective (Nyariki *et al.* 2009),

DOI: 10.4324/9781003230120-12

to cooperative corporations where the labourers act as shareholders and executives (Tortia 2018). *Werewolf* helps students explore the implications of information asymmetry and its potential impact on power balances.

Another important theme within *Werewolf* is the formation and impact of in-groups and out-groups (Tajfel 1979) – in this case with the out-group not fully aware who might be part of the secretive in-group, but fully aware of their own exclusion. This allows for the in-group (in this case the Werewolves) to build a much stronger rapport simply based on their shared secret and power over the out-group. In addition, there is a natural incentive for the in-group to remain secretive (i.e. loyal to the in-group). An interesting observation is that in some playthroughs, the in-group is perceived as being the Villagers (at least during the Day), and if the identity of the person who got killed is revealed, Werewolves might actually be incentivised to vote *against* other Werewolves if there is a rampant public suspicion of that player to avoid scrutiny themselves. This theme, if it emerges in the game, offers an interesting insight into scapegoating in a corporate setting (Roulet and Pichler 2020). Players may sacrifice those that 'appear' more guilty in order to ward off blame, and scapegoats may grudgingly accept this role because it might mean their group ends up winning in the end (they are properly incentivised).

Finally, this game is also useful to illustrate the importance of transparency and information access in government or business policy. As such, it lays a good foundation for understanding democratic institutions (like press freedom, public access to information, governance transparency, etc.) As Fenwick (2006) discusses, press freedom and the role of the media is vital in upholding universal human rights in a democratic setting. This allows the game to explore concepts like how trust is built in society, and morality under authoritarianism.

During the course of this chapter, instructions will refer to a 'Narrator'. This could be the educator, but even another student may play this role if they are familiar with the rules of the game.

12.2 Games Details

12.2.1 Key Skills

Information asymmetry, democracy and governance, trust and group power dynamics, ethics and morality under totalitarianism.

12.2.2 Group Size

12–25 students + 1 Narrator. Although groups larger than 25 could be played by printing more Werewolf cards and villager cards, the game can become quite lengthy and perhaps boring. The optimal number is 15–20 players.

12.2.3 Time

1.5 hours. One round can take as little as 30 minutes if properly managed by the Narrator, but three rounds are recommended.

12.2.4 Purpose (Learning Objectives)

1. To understand the power that a minority with information has over a majority with no information.
2. To understand the importance of press freedom, public access to information and transparent governance in a democracy or a democratic institution.
3. To understand one way in which trust is formed in a society and how tenuous (and unfounded) that trust may be.

12.2.5 Preparation and Setup

Students are set up preferably in a circle (or any other setup that allows the Narrator to access all players freely and noiselessly – for example, if the Narrator needs to climb over bags or chairs to reach a player, it is not ideal).

The Narrator has the following equipment:

- A stick or staff used for interacting with players
- Player cards
- The amount of Werewolves in play is determined by the size of the group. You should never have fewer than two Werewolves (the smallest playable group is ten players). The amount of Werewolves in play scale as follows:

    - 10–14 players = 2 Werewolves.
    - 15–19 players = 3 Werewolves; plus the Druid and Werhamster characters. For all smaller groups, leave these cards out entirely.
    - 20–25 players = 4 Werewolves, plus the Druid, Werhamster, Spellweaver and Cursed One characters. For all smaller groups, leave out the Spellweaver and Cursed One cards entirely.

This game does not require any technical support.

12.2.6 Instructions

This game pits the Werewolves against the Villagers. When all Villagers are eliminated, the Werewolves win and vice versa. Players are guided through the game by the Narrator, who can create a story around all the steps of the game to fully immerse players.

The game is divided into two phases: a Day phase and a Night phase. During the Night, all players' eyes are closed, and some players are woken by the Narrator. No player is allowed to ever speak during the Night. During the Day, all players may open their eyes and converse freely.

When the game starts, the Narrator will randomly choose a town Mayor and then instruct everyone to close their eyes for the first Night. All players will receive a secret character card (including the Mayor) which they may never reveal to any other player – the card should remain secret even when they have been eliminated from the game. Players may then quickly look at their character card, then close their eyes again. The Narrator will ask the two Lovers to open their eyes and identify each other and then close them again. Thereafter, the Narrator will ask all the Werewolves to open their eyes and again without making any noise, identify each other. The Werewolves then choose a player they wish to kill by indicating silently and communicating through head nodding and pointing – making no noise. For this very first Night, Werewolves cannot target the Mayor but are free to do so thereafter.

Players then get told that they can open their eyes, and the first Day begins. All subsequent Days and Nights follow the same pattern:

1. Day: The Narrator announces who has been killed during the Night.
2. Day: If the Mayor is still alive, skip this step. If the Mayor is dead, players nominate someone they think should be Mayor. Nominations should be supported by another player and people cannot self-nominate. Once three nominations have been made, Nominees have a few seconds to explain why they would be the best Mayor. Players then vote for the Mayor by putting one hand in the air, and the Narrator counts to three. On the third count, all players point to one of the three nominees they wish to vote for – they cannot change their votes after casting and should keep their hands still until all votes have been counted. The person with the most votes becomes the Mayor. In the case of a tie, the nominee who was not tied with anyone gets removed from the list of nominees and a fresh round of voting ensues. If there is still a tie, the previous (dead) Mayor breaks the tie.
3. Day: Players then identify up to three suspects they think may be Werewolves. Any accusations of suspicion need to be supported by another player. After three suspects have been identified, each suspect is given a few seconds to plead their defence to the group.
4. Day: After all defences have been heard, each player puts one hand in the air, and the Narrator counts to three. On the third count, all players point to one of the three suspects they wish to vote for – they cannot change their votes after casting and should keep their hands still until all votes have been counted. The Mayor puts two hands in the air, casting two votes.
5. Day: The person who received the most votes gets hanged by the townsfolk. In the case of a tie, the suspect who was not tied with anyone gets removed from the list of suspects and a fresh round of voting ensues. If there is still a tie, the Mayor breaks the tie.
6. Night: All players close their eyes, and characters are awakened in the following order. The Narrator can read these instructions exactly as written, but only the Narrator may speak, no one else. This order is also noted on the Narrator reference card under the resources:

A. The Medium opens their eyes, and the Narrator gives a thumbs up if the hanged person was a Werewolf, or a thumbs down if they were not.
B. The Spellweaver chooses another player to protect from death this Night and the next Day. This person can be targeted, but will not be killed.
C. The Druid is asked if they want to use their ability to resurrect a dead player in exchange for a living one.
D. Tell the Little Girl that they may open their eyes from now on during the Werewolf phase, but if they are seen by the Werewolves, the Werewolves only need to point them out, and the Little Girl instantly dies.
E. The Werewolves wake and decide on a new victim.
F. The Cursed One opens their eyes, and if they are the victim of the previous step, they become a Werewolf. All the Werewolves then wake up to identify one another, and no new victim is killed.
G. Tough-as-Nails opens up their eyes, and if they were the victim of step E, they are told that they have survived their first death. After surviving the first death, they are not reawakened and simply killed when targeted again.
H. The Werhamster wakes up, and if they were the victim in step E, they choose a Werewolf to kill before dying themselves. They are the only character that cannot be resurrected by the Druid.
I. The Seer is awakened and points to any player. The Narrator gives a thumbs up if that player is a Werewolf, or a thumbs down if that player is not a Werewolf.
J. The Thaumaturge is awakened, and the Narrator shows them the number of Werewolves left in the game.
K. Without saying anything out loud, the Narrator considers if one of the Lovers died, in which case the other lover will also be announced as dead in the morning.

The game resumes in this fashion until all Villagers are killed, or all Werewolves are killed. All eliminated players should still close their eyes at Night and may open them during the Day. But they may not speak or in any other way contribute to the game.

Since the game time of some players may be quite brief (they may be killed in the first Night), it is always best to play this game more than one round. Although the educator may choose to play the game as is for another two rounds (totalling three rounds), it is also possible to inspire minor behaviour changes in subsequent rounds based on the debriefing questions in Section 12.2.8.

12.2.7 Guidance

A list of things to watch out for with possible suggestions on how to mitigate against them. A list of helpful tips to make the session more effective.

One of the most important things to make the game work is the need for absolute silence during the Night phase. Even small sounds like moving an arm, or bumping against a neighbour may give away the secret of who the Werewolves are. It is therefore important to stress the need for silence very strongly – and if the silence is broken early on (for example, if one of the Werewolves speaks out loudly during the Night), rather reset the game entirely than continue.

Generally, the Day phases tend to be much longer than the nights since this is when the bulk of the negotiations and discussions take place.

In his rules for "Werewolf", Plotkin recommends that the first phase be Night and that there be an odd number of players (including the moderator). These specifications avoid tie votes for eliminations and ensure that the game will end dramatically on an elimination rather than anticlimactically with murder as a foregone conclusion.

The Narrator can use a stick/staff in order to more accurately point to potential targets during the Night phase since this allows for more silent indication. Also beware that the Narrator cannot move closer to anyone or speak consistently in any direction when communicating with the Werewolves, lest the townsfolk suspect in which general direction the Werewolves may be seated.

The game can be made more immersive and engaging when using storytelling and drama to take players through the phases. For example, after player Ntombi was killed by Werewolves during the Night, you can announce the victim by saying something like, "Last Night, many of you were woken by howls and yells, the pale moon shining through your windows. As you barred your doors in fear, you could hear the scratching of tallons walking down the street. This morning, as you open your window, you see the blood-smeared door of your beloved friend, Ntombi, and you know that she has been killed by the Werewolves. You are angry, and you rush outside, demanding to see the murderer hanged! Who do you think committed this heinous crime?!"

Players are very much allowed to lie about their characters. They are free to claim that they are a certain character to support an accusation or appeal to be Mayor. However, at no point may any player reveal their character card to prove their identity, even after their death.

Some character-specific guidance:

The Spellweaver each Night chooses a person they wish to protect. If this person is targeted by the Werewolves, the Narrator will not indicate this to the Werewolves. Ex., if the Spellweaver decides to protect player X, and the Werewolves decide to kill player X, the Narrator will accept their choice and continue. However, in the Day phase, the Narrator will simply announce that someone was attacked last Night, but strong magic spells protected them from death. In that way, the Werewolves don't know who protected their victim, nor does the victim (player X) know they were the target. The Spellweaver is allowed to choose to protect themselves using their power.

The Druid can only use their power once during the entire game. If the Druid dies before using their power, they <u>cannot</u> use it to bring themselves back to life. On the Day after the power was used, the Narrator can simply announce that through some dark ritual, player X has been brought back to life. The Narrator will then announce all the deaths that occurred that Night in no particular order, leaving the townsfolk unsure who died from Werewolf and who died from the Druid. It is possible for the Druid to inadvertently resurrect a Werewolf if they choose it.

The Tough-as-Nails character can survive one death only. If the character is hanged by the Villagers, it will die and be resurrected in the morning. In this way, the people may still suspect that the player who has been resurrected came back because of the Druid's work.

When the Werhamster kills a Werewolf, both deaths are revealed to the Villagers in no order the next Day. Villagers, therefore, do not fully know why they died, or who may have been what character.

When one of the Lovers dies, the death of the other lover can be announced thematically linked to the death of the first. For example, if player X died, and they were the lover of player Y, then the Narrator announces their death the next morning. If player X was hanged, then player Y's death could be announced as "and in the morning after that fateful hanging, everyone found the broken body of player Y, whose heart was broken long before her body perished beneath the dangling feet of her lover".

12.2.8 Debrief

QUESTIONS AFTER ROUND 1

The Villagers greatly outnumbered the Werewolves, yet the latter still won. Why?

How could the Villagers have better protected themselves against the Werewolves?

How did you know who you could trust? What informed the way you voted?

As a Werewolf, what was the most difficult thing for you in the game?

One researcher, Max Ventilla, noted that the voting patterns are an important sign of someone's motivations. If Villagers all keep and use voting records, they mostly end up winning. Would you agree?

QUESTIONS AFTER ROUND 3

What is the best way in which you can encourage others to trust you?

The game's designer, Dimma Davidoff, showed that if you play the game multiple times with the same group of people, you are more likely to be the 'winner' if you are known for honesty. That means it is better in the long run to be honest (and tell everyone you're a Werewolf) instead of concealing that fact. Do you think that is true?

If this was a country built on the premise of democracy, do you think this is truly democratic?

The majority of people want a Werewolf-free village, yet they ended up taking over because of information asymmetry. In what way could the village have better protected itself by implementing certain policies or procedures?

How important do you think press freedom and transparency are in a democracy?

What other lessons can we learn from the psychology of this game and how people act?

12.2.9 Handouts and Material

A printable version of the cards can be found for free at http://games.2ndordergaming.de/2011/10/05/at-last-my-printable-werewolf-game-is-here/.[2] You can also find many other versions printable for free.

Alternatively, a deck of playing cards can be used by assigning a different card to each character. The following is an example:

Medium: Ace of spades
Spellweaver: Ace of hearts

Druid: Ace of clubs
Tough-as-Nails: Ace of diamonds
Werhamster: Queen of spades
Seer: Queen of hearts
Cursed One: Queen of clubs
Little Girl: Queen of diamonds

12.3 Adaptation of the Games to a Different Context

A very large online community exists around the game, and many variants[2] have been developed since Mafia's original inception. The original Mafia basically only has townsfolk and mafiosa (Werewolves), with none of the other characters. This is a simpler variant, but one that is not as engaging to the townspeople.

There are also several online playable variants for groups, such as *Werewolves*, or *Among Us*, which is a space-themed game with a similar premise. Both are online multiplayer free-to-play games that could conceivably be used even in an online class setting.

There are also many card decks that have been developed with beautifully designed and high-quality cards and rules that slightly differ from those described here. You may also want to change, add or alter the roles in accordance with ideas you may find online based on other variants.

Notes

1 Andrew Plotkin first adapted the Mafia rules to Werewolf, which was a more culturally relevant imagery in the USA. The game has been used and studied at Princeton and several game theory studies have been published to consider the application of a *homo economicus* in the game, such as the study done by Braverman, Mark, Omid Etesami and Elchanan Mossel. "Mafia: A theoretical study of players and coalitions in a partial information environment." *The Annals of Applied Probability* 18, no. 3 (2008): 825–46.

2 Many versions of the game exist, and many printable variants can be downloaded free of charge online. There are also many affordable versions that come in neat packaging on high-quality cards. The version used in this chapter is based on the free downloadable version developed by user Wey Han-Tan. You can access it here: http://games.2ndordergaming.de/2011/10/05/at-last-my-printable-werewolf-game-is-here/.

Bibliography

Fenwick, H.M. and Phillipson, G. (2006). *Media freedom under the Human Rights Act*. Oxford: Oxford University Press.

Nyariki, D.M., Mwang'Ombe, A.W. and Thompson, D.M. (2009). Land-use change and livestock production challenges in an integrated system: the Masai-Mara ecosystem, Kenya. *Journal of Human Ecology*, 26(3), pp. 163–73.

Roulet, T. J. and Pichler, R. (2020). Blame game theory: scapegoating, whistleblowing and discursive struggles following accusations of organizational misconduct. *Journal of Special Education Technology*, pp. 15–24. https://doi.org/10.1177/0162634 340001500402.

Tajfel, H., Turner, J.C., Austin, W.G. and Worchel, S. (1979). An integrative theory of intergroup conflict. In: Austin, W. G. and Worchel, S., eds. *Organizational identity: a reader.* Monterey, CA: Brooks Cole, pp. 33–47.

Tortia, E.C. (2018). The firm as a common. Non-divided ownership, patrimonial stability and longevity of co-operative enterprises. *Sustainability*, 10(4), p. 1023.

13 Building up Trust and Rapport with Neuroscience Insights

Carola Hieker

13.1 Overview

Helping students to settle into the classroom and building a safe and trustful atmosphere is always a huge challenge for any lecturer. This exercise establishes an entertaining, friendly and open way of communicating with each other and at the same time fosters emotional intelligence. It can be used in any kind of lecture but would be especially useful in courses that focus on management or social science. It can be used with postgraduate and undergraduate students but also in adult learning. We have used it many times as an opener for leadership workshops all over the world and the feedback independent of the cultural background was always overwhelmingly positive.

So, what is the exercise about: the title of the exercise is called "Speculative Listening" as the participants are invited in small groups of three to share first impressions. Two people (person A and B) talk about the third person (person C) by 'answering' the questions they receive on the instruction sheet located in the material handouts. Answering means in this case they are speculating, making assumptions about person C without having any valid information. The third person (person C) is present and listening without showing any reactions/emotions to what is said. Person C listens carefully and might take some notes but gives no other input to the 'speculating' peers.

DOI: 10.4324/9781003230120-13

13.2 Games Details

13.2.1 Key Skills

Emotional intelligence, communication skills, building trust and rapport

13.2.2 Group Size

Any size, ideally at least nine participants, the group will be divided into small groups of three

13.2.3 Time

Around an hour (Around 30 to 40 minutes plus 15–20 minutes wrap up in plenary)

13.2.4 Purpose (Learning Objectives)

Participants will …

1. *get to know each other;*
2. *become aware of own judgements;*
3. *understand the importance of judgement/decision-making from an evolutionary perspective, as well as the danger of unconscious judgements;*
4. *find out what first impression they might make on other people and what triggers these first impressions;*
5. *learn about the three areas of the brain and in which part of the brain which decisions are made;*
6. *improve communication skills; and*
7. *build trust and have fun.*

13.2.5 Preparation and Setup

- Room – depending on group size, break-out rooms are needed
- Tech – no tech needed

13.2.6 Instructions

13.2.6.1 Group Size: 3

Find two other people in the room who ideally you have never met before and don't know anything about.

You are in groups of 3: person A, person B, person C. Now you take turns making assumptions about each other and sharing your first impressions. Person A and person B will start reflecting on the questions written on the instruction sheet. A and B make assumptions about person C, talk about person C while C is listening. Person C is asked not to show any emotions and keep a passive demeanour. Person C can take some notes about what he/she is hearing – e.g., assumptions made by A and B that are very accurate or maybe don't fit at all.

When the first round is finished (A and B exchange speculative answers to the questions on the instruction sheet) roles are changed – e.g., A becomes C.

When all participants have been 'person C', participants are asked to come back to the plenary. Depending on the group size, a disclosure is limited to some highlights or more information about what really fits well. Per participant, the disclosure should not be longer than 2 minutes as the rest of the group will otherwise get bored. Usually as a result the lecturer will find that most participants are surprised how well the peers speculated on person C's way of handling conflict. As some groups might be faster than others in finishing the 'speculations', the faster small group can use the 'waiting time' to start disclosing in their group of three. If groups feel the 'disclosure time' in plenary wasn't enough, they are encouraged to continue in small groups during a break.

13.2.6.2 Exercise: Speculative Listening

Person A - *"I think person C doesn't like conflict very much and tries to avoid a confrontation as long as possible".*
Person B - *"I agree".*
Person C - *"I can't say anything. But they are right…"*

13.2.7 Guidance

Separate groups
It is important that small groups don't sit too close to each other so that they cannot hear what's going on in the other groups. Break-out rooms would be great; otherwise, groups should be sent to different corners of the room or if possible, sit outside. Privacy for the small groups is key to the success of the exercise
Encouragement
Some groups find it very easy to start the exercise, while others are struggling. As facilitators, please walk around, encourage them just to start with one person and feel confident that the exercise gets easier while doing it.
Disclosure
Make sure that everybody has been 'person C' before disclosure starts.
Group size cannot be divided by three
Groups of four are possible but need to be faster per person. Lecturers should watch them, and if one small group is already finished, do not hesitate to change group members during the process. It is important that everybody has been person C during the exercise.

13.2.8 Debrief

Once the groups are back in plenary, the following debrief questions can be asked to get the participants to reflect on the exercise.

What did you like about the exercise?
Raise your hand if your group mates described you with 100% accuracy?

Raise your hand if your group mates described you with 80% accuracy?
Raise your hand if your group mates described you with 50% accuracy?
Raise your hand if your group mates did not describe you at all?
Share one highlight of the exercise which was accurate

Note: Usually the responses to the raise hand poll are around 80%–90% of accuracy, and participants will tend to express their surprise at how this could be possible.

Examples of participants' feedback on the exercise:

- *This is amazing how well they characterised me even though we have never met before.*
- *This was really fun.*
- *I would never thought how quickly you can build up rapport.*
- *I feel I know this person really well now.*
- *Most of their guesses around the way I live were wrong but, in a way, they described the life I probably would have now if wasn't married with children.*
- *Time was over so fast … I just got into it.*

13.2.9 Further Lecturing: Input on Gut Feeling, Decision-Making and the Human Brain

If this opener is used for students in management, social science, psychology, etc., it is a great opportunity to introduce some background information on neuroscience.

1. Decisions and the structure of the brain

Lecturers might want to explain the different parts of the brain and how they influence decision-making. In 1990, physician and neuroscientist Paul MacLean provided a concept that our human brains are composed of three parts:

1. The reptilian brain, composed of the basal ganglia (striatum) and brainstem, is involved with primitive drives related to thirst, hunger, sexuality and territoriality, as well as habits and procedural memory (like putting your keys in the same place every day without thinking about it or riding a bike).
2. The mammalian brain or limbic system, including the hypothalamus, hippocampus, amygdala and cingulate cortex, is the centre of our motivation, emotions, and memory, including behaviour such as building up rapport and bonding.
3. The key focus of the reptilian brain with support of the limbic system is to survive and decide what needs to be done – e.g., to fight, flight or pretend to be dead. These decisions are made before the neocortex is activated and are not conscious and reflected decisions.
4. The neocortex (new brain), enables language, abstraction, reasoning and planning. Here rational and reflected decisions are made.

Building up Trust and Rapport 139

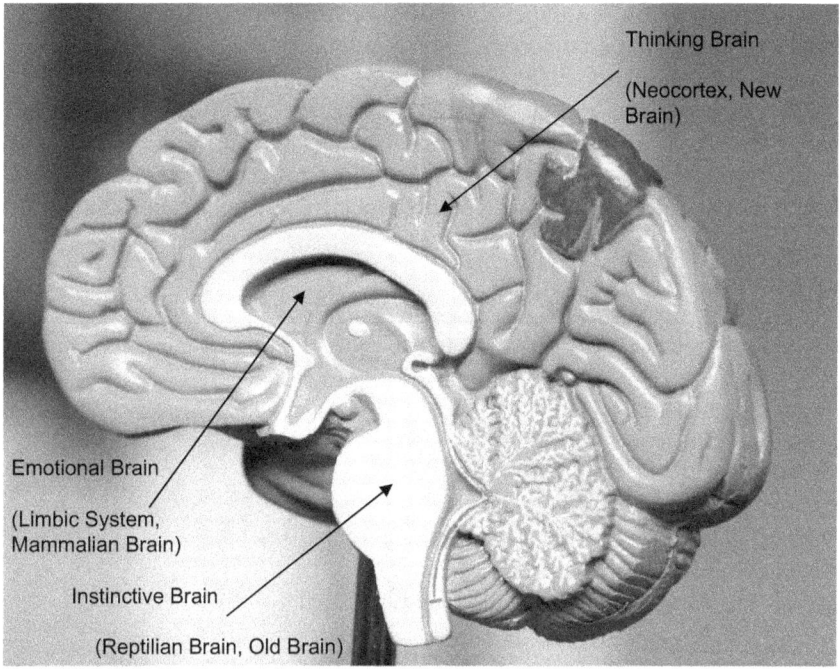

Figure 13.1 The three parts of the brain described: thinking, emotional and instinctive.

Photo by https://unsplash.com/@averey

2. Mirror Neurons

A **mirror** neuron is a neuron that fires both when a human being acts and when the human being observes the same action performed by another. Thus, the neuron "**mirrors**" the behaviour of the other, as though the observer were itself acting. Such **neurons** have been directly observed in human and primate species, and birds.

These mirror neurons help us to understand what's going on with the other person and are incredibly important in evolution to survive. Due to the mirror neurons, our reptile brain and mammal brain judge other people in a millisecond and make the decision to fight, flight or pretend to be dead.

13.2.9.1 What Happens During the Exercise?

In this exercise, participants are asked to follow their gut feeling and pick up information the activated mirror neurons send. As these are not reflected judgements, most of the decisions are made in the two 'older' brains, the instinctive brain and the emotional brain. A process which is always happening, as these brains are always sending information but are usually overlapped by other rational thinking in the neocortex. This doesn't mean that the assumptions person A and person B develop are right, but especially when it comes to evaluating a person's way of handling conflict, the instinctive and emotional brain adds valuable information.

Of course, our decisions about people can as well be influenced by our own memories – e.g., if person C reminds the others of somebody. Giving more input on neuroscience helps students to understand how important it is to become aware of their own judgements and critically reflect on them.

13.2.10 Handouts and Material

Associative Listening: persons 1 and 2 to make the following assumptions about person 3

Origin of family?

Learning style?

How did he/she behave as a child?

Current living situation and life situation?

Does he/she have hobbies? What are they?

Does he/she drive a car? What type?

Does he/she have secret passions/interests? What are they?

What are his/her typical character traits?

How does he/she handle conflict?

What does he/she like about studying?

What he/she dislikes about being a student?

What drives him/her nuts?

Copyright material from Hirani & Varin 2003, *Supporting Adult Learners through Games and Interactive Teaching,* Routledge

14 Design Thinking for Communication, Planning and Problem-Solving

Kasia Hanula

EMPATHIZE
DEFINE
IDEATE
PROTOTYPE
TEST

14.1 Overview

Design thinking is not a new phenomenon, but in recent years, it has gained popularity in multiple areas (business, design, education, just to name a few). Design thinking as a mindset allows for finding a creative solution to complex problems, therefore there is a clear value in applying design thinking methodology in education and advanced training as it will develop the skills that are crucial to successfully face the future. This approach will enable the delivery of learner-centred education, with the focus on addressing authentic problems that the learner may encounter. An additional benefit of bringing the design thinking process to education is the human-centric approach through the focus on learners' abilities and talents as well as individualised skills development. Design thinking process builds on idea generation, prototyping, testing and failing. The beauty of the design process is the value of the experiences gained during the process and not solely on creating the final solution. Design thinking is not a curriculum but rather a problem-solving creative process rooted in empathy, where the learning happens through the process. The games applied and used are structured in a way that gives full flexibility for the facilitators/teachers to create the spaces, lessons and activities plans that stimulate learning. The matter of individual engagement and consequent recognition of one's own actions become more explicit through gamification as students respond positively to that by showing higher indexes on factors like teamwork, questioning, cooperation, autonomy, among

DOI: 10.4324/9781003230120-14

others. All the games presented in this chapter can be used as a set to teach the design thinking process or can be played separately to develop key skills. If the games are used for the design thinking process, then the teams should remain the same for all of it. This chapter lays out between one and three games for each of the five pillars illustrated in the following design thinking process.

14.2 Games Details

Figure 14.1 shows the five-stage process of design thinking. This section outlines multiple games, each relating to one of the five stages.

Empathise: 1 game
Define: 2 games
Ideate: 3 games
Prototype: 2 games
Test: 1 game

14.2.1 Empathise

14.2.1.1 Game: Empathy Map

14.2.1.1.1 KEY SKILLS

Emotional intelligence, observation, communication, active listening

14.2.1.1.2 GROUP SIZE

Any – two to five people per group

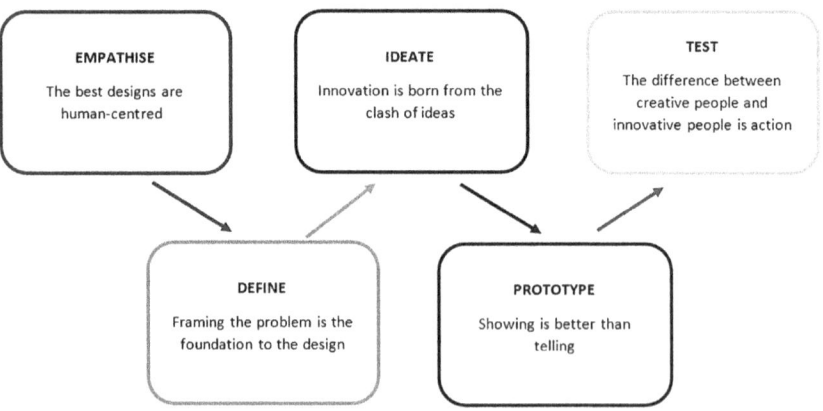

Figure 14.1 Design thinking process.

14.2.1.1.3 TIME

Approximately 25 minutes (depending on how well you understand the stakeholder and the context)

14.2.1.1.4 PURPOSE (LEARNING OBJECTIVES)

1. Understanding different audiences (consumers, groups that we want to influence/help, remote workers, people with disabilities, etc.) within the given context or ecosystem
2. Identify gaps in the understanding of the situation that you were not aware of
3. Improve communication and observation skills

14.2.1.1.5 PREPARATION AND SETUP

Paper sheet or drawing board to allow for visualisation.

14.2.1.1.6 GUIDANCE

To start, you need to decide on the subject and the scope of your empathy map (who are you mapping and what is your goal).

In the design thinking process, you are solving "wicked" problems for a certain group of people.

Alternatively, you could use a persona – a fictional archetype of a stakeholder (comprising all the features – i.e., elder women living in the rural area, businesspeople working in a big city, etc.).

14.2.1.1.7 INSTRUCTIONS

In the middle of the sheet/table draw a person, and give this person some identifying features (name, job title, background, physical features, family situation, living conditions, etc.). Think about this person as a real person that you met or saw on the street. You can draw more characteristics to make this person more real. The more details you can include the better you will be able to project yourself into the experiences of that person and empathise with him/her, which is the aim of this exercise.

What are the main questions you have for the person or what problem you are trying to solve for them? Is there anything in their life you are trying to understand? Write down all the information you find relevant.

Divide the circle into sections that represent aspects of that person's sensory experience. What are they thinking, feeling, saying, doing, hearing? Label the appropriate sections on the image.

Now step in the person's shoes. Try to emerge yourself in the person's experience/empathise with them. Focus on the context you want to understand. Based on that, start filling the diagram – i.e., "seeing" section could be a busy road, cars and traffic, in "saying" what the person could be saying, what thoughts they may have. Try not to put yourself into the person's shoes, be perceptive and try to really understand the person's perspective so you can better understand and empathise with the situation to solve the problem for them.

Review the map. Step back and ask others to review what you came up with. Ask others to make suggestions, add details and provide additional perspectives.

14.2.1.1.8 DEBRIEF

Empathy Mapping is a process that helps you to identify the thoughts and feelings of a particular group on a specific issue by making us "step in their shoes" and therefore empathise with them to find the solution that meets their needs.

Effective Empathy Mapping requires you to

- *identify your subject,*
- *collect qualitative data on your subject's perceptions of the situation,*
- *work with the others to build a map and*
- *reflect on your findings and draw conclusions.*

14.2.2 Define

14.2.2.1 Game 1 (Icebreaker): The Single Question

14.2.2.1.1 KEY SKILLS

Communication, critical thinking, flexibility

14.2.2.1.2 GROUP SIZE

Any – two to five people per group

14.2.2.1.3 TIME

15–20 minutes

14.2.2.1.4 PURPOSE (LEARNING OBJECTIVES)

1. Adaptability and asking the right question to solve the problem

14.2.2.1.5 MATERIALS NEEDED

None

14.2.2.1.6 INSTRUCTIONS

Divide participants into teams and pose a challenge: If they could ask only one question to discover a person's suitability or needs for *insert a topic here,* what would it be?

Design Thinking 145

14.2.2.1.7 DEBRIEF

This activity follows the idea expressed by Einstein: "If I had an hour to solve a problem and my life depended on the solution, I would spend the first 55 minutes determining the proper question to ask ... for once I know the proper question, I could solve the problem in less than five minutes".

This game demonstrates the importance of asking the right questions and also highlights different priorities. It is a great way to get groups talking and thinking together to define the challenge.

14.2.2.2 Game 2: Draw the Problem

14.2.2.2.1 KEY SKILLS

Problem-solving, strategy, communication, creativity, teamwork

14.2.2.2.2 GROUP SIZE

Any – two to five people per group

14.2.2.2.3 TIME

30 minutes

14.2.2.2.4 PURPOSE (LEARNING OBJECTIVES)

1. Problems can be difficult to define (especially wicked problems in the design thinking process); therefore, this exercise helps to focus on the core of the problem and what really matters.
2. It helps participants to engage with the purpose.
3. It creates understanding between participants working to solve the same problem.

14.2.2.2.5 PREPARATION AND SETUP

Room set up as smaller work stations (reception style)

14.2.2.2.6 MATERIALS NEEDED

Sheets of paper, markers/pencils

14.2.2.2.7 INSTRUCTIONS

Each team should have one big sheet of paper to draw on. After discussing the findings of game one (single question defining the problem), ask the participants to think and write a list of things that helped them to solve the problem.

After a few minutes of thinking, ask the participants to start drawing the pictures of the problem, it can be a single item or multiple items that relate to the problem they are trying to solve. The format of the drawing is completely up to the team members. The drawing should help in explaining the problem.

When all participants are finished, the teams should post their drawings on the wall and explain them to each other. After the exercise, the group should look at the similarities and differences and work towards a joint understanding of what the problem is by reflecting on the different points included by them in the drawing.

To make things more complicated. Teams may be asked to rotate after 5–10 minutes to finish the drawing of the different teams. This allows for additional aspects to the problem-solving. After the rotation, each team is asked to present, and the other contributing teams can ask questions or comment on why they drew certain things.

14.2.2.2.8 DEBRIEF

The aim of this exercise is a problem definition that engages participants in defining the challenge in a simplified form. It will bring the group together, helping them understand a common purpose and clarifying ways of working and communicating.

14.2.3 Ideate

14.2.3.1 Game 1: Unfinished Artwork

14.2.3.1.1 KEY SKILLS

Communication, creativity, abstract thinking, problem-solving

14.2.3.1.2 GROUP SIZE

Any – two to five people per group

14.2.3.1.3 TIME

15–25 minutes

14.2.3.1.4 PURPOSE (LEARNING OBJECTIVES)

1. Building comfort with constraints
2. Removing creativity blocks

14.2.3.1.5 PREPARATION AND SETUP

None

14.2.3.1.6 MATERIALS NEEDED

Piece of paper

14.2.3.1.7 INSTRUCTIONS

One person from the team draws on the pieces of paper (as many as there are team members) – a random (simple) shape.

Then the person who drew the shape hands over one of the pieces of paper to the remaining team member, with the task to finish the drawing in either an abstract or realistic manner that relates to the problem the team is working on.

Give everyone a few minutes to see what they draw. Speed is key; they should not overthink just draw "intuitively".

When the time is up, each team member should share their artwork with the group.

14.2.3.1.8 DEBRIEF

This exercise allows for stimulating the creative part of our brain for problem-solving. This is perfect for building comfort with constraints, which helps to focus ideas.

14.2.3.2 Game 2: All the News

14.2.3.2.1 KEY SKILLS

Creativity, team building, communication, feedback

14.2.3.2.2 GROUP SIZE

Any – two to five people per group

14.2.3.2.3 TIME

20 minutes

14.2.3.2.4 PURPOSE (LEARNING OBJECTIVES)

1. Boosting creativity
2. Seeing the big picture

14.2.3.2.5 MATERIALS NEEDED

Newspapers, sheets of paper, pens, blackboard

14.2.3.2.6 INSTRUCTIONS

Each person in the team is tasked to create different headlines from the future when the issue they are working on is no longer a problem. They can create as many headlines as they want.

The persons in the team can work together to collaborate on the headlines.

After some time, everyone shares their headline ideas with the rest of the participants and receives feedback. They also look at what steps/actions could cause a positive development in addressing the problem.

14.2.3.3 Game 3: Six Thinking Hats

14.2.3.3.1 KEY SKILLS

Decision-making, communication, creativity

14.2.3.3.2 GROUP SIZE

Any – two to five people per group

14.2.3.3.3 TIME

20–45 minutes

14.2.3.3.4 PURPOSE (LEARNING OBJECTIVES)

1. The method encourages participants to review all possible points of view.
2. This method enables the creation of collaborative teamwork that looks at the problem from a 360° view, which enables them to take the right decisions easily and with complete awareness of the situation.
3. Team collaboration and communication are being developed as the participants avoid lengthy debates and disagreements focusing on finding constructive solutions.
4. Universal method to deal with complex problems and creativity blocks (can be used by teams and individuals).

14.2.3.3.5 PREPARATION AND SETUP

1. Dividing participants into teams
2. Explanation of the different colours of the hats:

Blue: process

This hat allows for the process setting. The team will decide on the objectives, structuring the conversation and agreeing on the outcomes and next steps.

White: information

The white hat allows the team to focus on the big picture through taking an external perspective. Wearing this hat requires collecting and analysing the data available about the problem you face to identify gaps and opportunities.

Yellow: possibility

The yellow hat allows for spotting opportunities. In this phase, the team should feel free to present ideas that may be unrealistic. The aim is to avoid questioning ("but") or negating. Instead, the team should freely share their views ("what if?"). The participants should create a supportive environment, building trust and collaboration.

Black: risk

This is the hat of caution, useful for spotting inconsistencies and weaknesses. This is a pessimist's hat that allows the team to run a risk assessment. The team should look at what is working and what isn't and weigh the benefits and risks of the new approach.

Red: emotion

The red hat is concerned with intuition and emotion. Stakeholders wearing the red hat can take an emotional view, prioritising 'gut instincts' or how they feel about a particular avenue or decision or idea.

Green: creativity

Green hat thinking is about bringing new ideas to the table. The wilder, the better, focus on exploring new ideas. The purpose here is to explore what 'movement' such an idea can generate – what traction and positive results.

14.2.3.3.6 MATERIALS NEEDED

Different coloured hats or scarves, pieces of paper to diversify the different views, notebooks

14.2.3.3.7 INSTRUCTIONS

The whole group usually has to wear the same colour hat at the same time – it's not one hat per person.

The goal is constructive decision-making, so everyone needs to agree to wear each hat and to play by the rules.

Starting hat is always blue.

The teams agree to make suggestions and contribute to the ideas that correspond to the hat colour (putting other ideas on the side). There is a need to free flow ideas. Everyone needs to remember that they may change the point of view when "wearing another hat".

The ideas corresponding to each hat colour should be written down.

14.2.3.3.8 DEBRIEF

The 'six thinking hats' technique is primarily a group decision-making tool, designed to structure meetings and brainstorms to be as effective as possible.

14.2.4 Prototyping

14.2.4.1 Game 1: Storyboard

14.2.4.1.1 KEY SKILLS

Decision-making, communication, creativity

14.2.4.1.2 GROUP SIZE

Any – two to five people per group

14.2.4.1.3 TIME

45 minutes to 1.5 hour

14.2.4.1.4 PURPOSE (LEARNING OBJECTIVES)

1. Participants need to envision and describe an ideal future (or any topic) in sequence with pictures and words.
2. Participants learn to see the steps that lead to solving the problems and finding solutions.

14.2.4.1.5 PREPARATION AND SETUP

Spaces to place big sheets of paper for drawing

14.2.4.1.6 MATERIALS NEEDED

sheets of paper, pencils/markers, stands

14.2.4.1.7 INSTRUCTIONS

The storyboard starts with the story. The participants need to identify a character (persona), a setting and a plot (elements from empathise phase). The participants' assignment is to visually describe the topic and narrate it to the group.

The team should agree on what is the ideal future they are aiming for, determine what steps need to be taken and draw each step in a sequence (one scene per sheet). Combine quick sketches with speech and thought bubbles, action bursts, captions and narration.

The team should share the story they just created.

After all the groups have presented, ask what's inspiring in what they heard. Summarise any recurring themes and ask for observations, insights, and 'aha's' about the stories.

14.2.4.1.8 DEBRIEF

Walt Disney is credited for this activity. His need to animate Steamboat Willie *in 1928 led to the process of storyboarding – a story told in sequence on a wall covered with a special kind of board. He found it to be an effective way to track progress and improve a story.*

14.2.4.2 Game 2: Practical Creators

14.2.4.2.1 KEY SKILLS

Public speaking, creativity, teamwork

14.2.4.2.2 GROUP SIZE

5–20 participants

14.2.4.2.3 TIME

45 minutes to 1.5 hour

14.2.4.2.4 PURPOSE (LEARNING OBJECTIVES)

1. Participants learn how to visualise desired outcomes (starting from 3D models, to better global supply chains, inclusive companies, landscapes and city designs, etc.)

14.2.4.2.5 PREPARATION AND SETUP

Space so that the team can easily collaborate, move and exchange

14.2.4.2.6 MATERIALS NEEDED

Sheets of paper, post-its, scissors, modelling clay, magazines, index cards, pieces of wood, etc. (any supply available to allow them to prototype it can also be stones, leaves, ropes, plastic tops)

14.2.4.2.7 INSTRUCTIONS

Teams should look at the problem they tried to solve and discuss what and how they could contribute to the solution.

Tell the participants that they should build a 3D model of their solution. The prototype can be a thing but also a place, building, landscape – anything they may find necessary to address the problem.

The participants should have approximately 20–30 minutes to brainstorm what they want to do. After that, they should start constructing the model.

After the team finishes building the model, they should develop a one-sentence statement on what they created.

Different teams should present their prototypes to each other.

14.2.4.2.8 DEBRIEF

Through prototyping, the participants will make the thinking and problem-solving process into a more sensory experience.

It's useful (and downright fun) because it lets players imagine the future and act to create a first version of it.

All successful ventures start with a vision and some small, initial effort towards crystallisation.

14.2.5 Test

14.2.5.1 Game – Fire Drill

14.2.5.1.1 KEY SKILLS

Public speaking, creativity, feedback, critical thinking

14.2.5.1.2 GROUP SIZE

Up to ten people

14.2.5.1.3 TIME

1 hour

14.2.5.1.4 PURPOSE (LEARNING OBJECTIVES)

1. To finish the design thinking process, we need to test the idea from the prototyping stage
2. For the team to think through assumptions and obstacles and try to see if the idea they worked on can withhold testing

14.2.5.1.5 PREPARATION AND SETUP

Possibly a space/stage for presenting and showcasing the prototype

14.2.5.1.6 MATERIALS NEEDED

None

14.2.5.1.7 INSTRUCTIONS

The team is preparing a presentation of their prototype, explaining in as much detail as they need, the process and the final solution 'designed' by them.

The other teams are actively listening to the presentation and try to challenge the prototype by providing different sometimes impossible scenarios (i.e., how would you charge it if there is no electricity, etc.)

After listening to the comments and questions, the prototyping team should have enough information to improve the prototype. Following this, a reflective discussion about both common and uncommon approaches should yield a list of possible solutions to be explored further.

The role of the other team members is not to criticise the idea but to provide constructive feedback.

14.2.5.1.8 DEBRIEF

To create something new, we need to challenge constraints and listen to other points of view.
This is also a good exercise to practice giving and receiving feedback.

14.3 Adaptation of the Games to a Different Context

The above games are being modified from various design thinking, facilitation and coaching tools. They can be used in various contexts (schools, businesses, non-governmental organisations (NGOs), etc.). The idea is that the games are allowing the players to reach out to the most creative ways of problem-solving and develop skills such as communication, presentation and active listening without really focusing on it. The learning through the games is more 'incidental', and the students have much more possibility to learn the soft skills without even realising that they are doing so. The materials used in the games can be modified as to the availability in the given context as they build on creativity and adaptability of both teacher/facilitator and the students.

The games in this chapter were adapted by the author from multiple tools and facilitation workshops to fit into the design thinking curriculum that can be used in schools, NGOs and social enterprises. Special mention needs to be given to:

- IDEO https://www.ideo.com/eu
- Gamestorming – James Macanufo
- Design for Growth Jeanne M. Liedtka
- Stanford d.school
- Coaching tools from Neuro-Linguistic Programming and facilitation techniques

15 Using an Experiential Activity to Teach Customer Discovery in Entrepreneurship

Demilade Oluwasina

15.1 Overview

Customer discovery is an important concept for any new start-up or entrepreneur seeking to grow a sustainable business. In spite of this, many entrepreneurs still fail because they do not have a clear approach to conducting customer discovery that provides the insights that will help them deliver a validated solution to the market. The experiential in this chapter is designed to model the real-life approach for carrying out the customer discovery exercise. Through the experiential, students will complete the same steps that they will be completing when going out to survey actual customers.

Experiential learning is a way to simulate real-life scenarios that allow learners to learn by doing and to be able to reflect on what they have learned. Through these methods, learners are immersed in the process and activity and are able to gather practical and relevant knowledge and skills as they interact with the scenarios and activities. According to Kolb, there are four stages of experiential learning which include concrete experience, reflective observation, abstract conceptualisation and active experimentation (Kolb 1984). In themselves, these different stages represent components of a learning cycle, and learners can enter into the cycle at any point in the process. Importantly, the experiential approach aligns more closely and prepares students for the real world, where they will spend their time beyond the institution; consequently, the goal is simulating real-world experience.

There has been a lot written about customer discovery; however, one of the most fundamental and widely accepted approaches comes from Steven Blank

DOI: 10.4324/9781003230120-15

in his book, *The Four Steps to the Epiphany*. According to him, the customer discovery process is comprised of four main steps, including stating the problem hypothesis, testing the problem hypothesis, testing the product concept and verifying the product/solution (Blank 2013). This experiential draws heavily from Steven Blank's work as well as from other contributors who have accepted and expanded on his original work.

Some of the key activities in the game that further develop students' skills include creating and testing hypotheses, interviewing and active listening. These skills will form a foundation for learners in becoming entrepreneurs that are market-oriented and who have proven frameworks for discovering their markets and creating fitting products.

With the growing prioritisation of entrepreneurship education all over the world, there has been an equally important discourse on the most innovative and effective methods for equipping students with entrepreneurial skills and competencies. Applied learning approaches remain some of the most-effective ways to develop students with the capacity to be effective as entrepreneurs. Through experiential learning, students do not merely acquire theoretical knowledge but are able to move towards development of entrepreneurial skills by participating actively in the learning process (Cooper 2004). The experiential is therefore designed to help students learn entrepreneurial skills through practice and reflection. In particular, the customer discovery experiential activity is relevant for different kinds of entrepreneurs, as most products whether from new or established companies that do not go through the customer development process tend to fail. Students will therefore be able to not only practice the skills of customer discovery but also be able to observe and evaluate its contribution to the entrepreneurship process.

The customer discovery experiential activity can be used at different levels of education including high schools, as well as undergraduate and graduate programmes at higher institutions. In addition, this experiential learning activity can be used by adults as well as individuals in the workforce and in organisations to drive effective learning outcomes that result in improved job performance and problem-solving for the organisation. Experiential learning is increasingly the focus of analysis in workplace learning and community-based education (Fenwick 2001).

15.2 Games Details

15.2.1 Key Skills

Hypothesis development and testing, customer interviews, prototyping product development, iteration

15.2.2 Group Size

Any even number – learners working in pairs

15.2.3 Time

1 hour 30 minutes – inclusive of experiential activity and debrief

15.2.4 Purpose (Learning Objectives)

1. To practice and understand the importance of customer discovery and the different stages it is composed of
2. To practice interviewing customers and understand how to have unbiased conversations with potential customers
3. To demonstrate how to integrate feedback from customers into the product development process for improvement

15.2.5 Preparation and Setup

There will be two main groups in the class:

> Scenario 1: the Entrepreneurs/Product Developers (Group A) and the Potential customers (Group B).
> Scenario 2: the Entrepreneurs/Product Developers (Group B) and the Potential customers (Group A).

Materials required include the following:

- Role description brief for Entrepreneurs/Product Developer
- Role description brief for Potential Customer
- Interview worksheets

15.2.6 Instructions

Student groups will take turns in this experiential activity to step into the shoes of Entrepreneurs and Product Developers trying to meet the needs of potential customers. This activity will go through the different steps that are required for customer discovery. Customer discovery is important for new businesses – the profitability and longevity of the business depend on knowing who its customers are, knowing what they want and how they want to acquire it, as well as how they will pay for it. As highlighted earlier, both Group A and B will be able to give feedback to each other in a reflective manner to highlight how well they performed in customer discovery.

Customer discovery involves creating a hypothesis about a problem and solution, testing that hypothesis, testing the product idea and then deciding how to move forward based on the insights received from potential customers.

Scenario Brief 1:
The potential customer (Group B) is a recruiter who is finding it difficult to secure skilled tech talent for companies for which the recruiter hires. The Product

Developer/Entrepreneur (Group A) will work to develop solutions for the potential customer's challenge.

<u>Scenario Brief 2:</u>
The potential customer (Group A) is a student who is struggling to make successful Graduate School applications. The Product Developer/Entrepreneur (Group B) will work to develop solutions for the potential customer's challenge.

During the different turns, the members of the group/pair will work through their brief. The Product Developer/Entrepreneur will work on developing a hypothesis they want to test as well as identifying questions they would like to ask the potential customer. The potential customer on the other hand will note down what success will look like for them in the light of solving the problem that they are facing.

After both rounds have been completed, the groups/pairs will give each other feedback on how well they were able to listen to the customer and absorb what had been communicated in developing their product. Students will then debrief the activity overall to see how the different components of the customer discovery process are carried out.

Steps of the Customer Discovery Process:

1. Write out your product/solution hypothesis and assumptions.
2. Test your hypotheses by interviewing potential customers.
3. Use the feedback received to refine/define a product concept/prototype and test again.
4. Test the product concept with the audience, incorporate feedback and determine next steps.

Read the brief outlined above to the students.

Divide students into pairs (e.g., if there are 24 students, there should be 12 pairs).

The pairs of students will be further labelled the Group As and Group Bs. In this case, there will be six Group As and six Group Bs.

As and Bs will be further matched together to form clusters. We will end up with six clusters of four people (one pair of Group A matched with one pair of Group B).

The briefs for the respective sides will be handed over to them and both groups will take time apart to review their brief and complete the steps assigned to them – 10 minutes.

For Group A in scenario 1, students will need to develop their hypothesis (one to three hypotheses will be sufficient for this experiential activity) around the problem and complete an interview worksheet.

Using the interview worksheet, Group A in scenario 1 will test their hypothesis by interviewing Group B to seek validation and feedback – 10 minutes.

After the time for the initial interview is up and Group A in scenario 1 has collected more details on the problems faced, Group A will put up a product concept, which will also be subject to testing with Group B. This product concept can be represented as a low-fidelity prototype/sketch for the next step – 5 minutes.

Having utilised insights that were gathered to develop the product concept earlier, Group A in scenario 1 will again test the product concept (prototype) with Group B to see how the product fits with the needs and preferences of Group B – 5 minutes.

Students in Group A for scenario 1 will then take the feedback they have received from Group B and note down next steps and what they now understand the problem and solution to be – 5 minutes.

Ideally, these steps can be carried out over and again until there is a good alignment with the needs of the customer.

This will mark the end of the first round, and then students in both groups will switch roles and repeat the entire process all over, this time with scenario 2 – 35 minutes.

After both groups are done going through the discovery steps, they will note down their experiences being on both sides of the challenge and evaluate how well they believe the other group performed, especially as Entrepreneurs/Product Developers in the interview and listening processes – 5 minutes.

Students will gather together as a class to debrief the experience, which can be led by the instructor or class facilitator – 15 minutes.

15.2.7 Guidance

Students in the role of Product Developer/Entrepreneur should think carefully and write down the questions that they want to ask the potential customer ahead of the interviews.

Students may be nervous about interviewing. Let them know it is okay to ask exploratory questions to develop common ground with the potential customer.

The students in the role of potential customer will need to imagine themselves as the customers in the scenario given and respond to questions asked not just as students but as the actual potential customers in that scenario.

The students playing the potential customers can define what success looks like in terms of the solution that will best address their problem in line with the suggestion in their brief.

As mentioned, playing both roles will give students an opportunity to experience customer discovery from an observation, as well as practical approach.

Students who are Product Developers/Entrepreneurs should ensure to write a clear hypothesis about their problem, as well as solution. A simple framing could be: Our idea solves [insert problem] by [insert solution]. Assumptions being made should also be captured.

Questions asked during the interviews should be open-ended in order to allow potential customers to describe the situation better in unbiased ways.

15.2.8 Debrief

Once all students are back in the main class, the following debrief questions can be asked to get the participants to reflect on the activity.

How successful would you consider the customer discovery process that you just engaged in? Here, the Team Bs can give feedback on how well the Team As were able to understand and represent their needs.

What made the customer discovery successful or otherwise? What did each group do well and what could they have done better?

Which of the steps in the process was most impactful to the end product in your opinion and why?

Which of the steps in the process was most challenging and why?

What did you learn from being on both sides of the challenge/activity?

How did you develop the questions you asked the potential customers, and how helpful were they in better understanding the needs and context of the customer?

How might the product development process have turned out if you did not engage in the customer discovery process?

How did you choose/prioritise the feedback to incorporate into your product concept development?

What will you do differently and what steps might you spend more time on if you were to do this again?

Why is customer discovery important in developing products and businesses?

How would you approach this differently when approaching or carrying out customer discovery with individuals whom you do not necessarily know like your colleagues?

In addition to the debrief questions here, the facilitator or lecturer can help ground students and learners in translating their experiences into meaningful concepts that can be described and to further discuss the importance of these concepts in the context of entrepreneurship.

Finally, beyond this one session, students can be supported and guided to apply the same approaches to actual live projects, thereby coming to the point of active experimentation.

15.2.9 Handouts and Material

15.2.9.1 Role Briefs

Role	Description and Responsibilities
Entrepreneurs/ Product Developers	In this role, you will act as the entrepreneurs who are seeking to develop a solution/product in response to a problem that has been identified. The problem will be based on a scenario. Group A will play this role for scenario 1, Group B will play this role for scenario 2. As a first step, write out the hypothesis that you will be testing, including the problem and the potential solution you want to deploy to address it. Also, include whatever assumptions you are making. Secondly, use the interview worksheet to think through the types of questions you want to ask and fill in insights that you get from the interview process with the potential customer. After your initial interview, you will update your product concept, which you will then test again with the potential customers group.

Copyright material from Hirani & Varin 2003, *Supporting Adult Learners through Games and Interactive Teaching*, Routledge

Potential Customers	In this role, you will act as the potential customers who are affected by the problem and are seeking an appropriate solution to this problem. The problem will be based on a scenario. Group B will play this role for scenario 1, Group A will play this role for scenario 2. You will need to put yourself in the shoes of the actual persons that experience this problem and want to see it solved. Before the interview, along with your colleague in the group, make notes on criteria your final solution should fulfil in order for it to be satisfactory for you. On that basis, aim to give candid feedback to the interviewing group as they seek to understand the problem and offer a solution.

15.2.10 Interview Worksheet

Interviewer:

Customer:

Date:

Notes: Make this a conversation as much as it is an interview. The goal is to avoid the interviewee being in a position where they feel that they have to impress you with their answers. You want them to give you answers that are as honest as possible. Therefore, you can start out with questions to build rapport before the main recorded questions.

Ask the questions but also observe and listen for peculiar words and mannerisms with which the interviewees respond to your questions.

Questions	Observations
1. How would you describe your role and what you do as a recruiter?	*Observe key words, emphasis and behaviours that are used when the interviewee responds.*
2. What does success look like for you in your role and in the key tasks you perform?	*Observe key words, emphasis and behaviours that are used when the interviewee responds.*

Copyright material from Hirani & Varin 2003, *Supporting Adult Learners through Games and Interactive Teaching*, Routledge

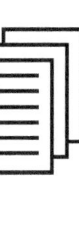

3. What are the greatest challenges you face in achieving the 'success' described in question 2?

Observe key words, emphasis and behaviours that are used when the interviewee responds.

4. When was the last time these challenges occurred, and how did you attempt to solve them?

Observe key words, emphasis and behaviours that are used when the interviewee responds.

5. Can you describe some solutions you tried out in addressing these challenges?

Observe key words, emphasis and behaviours that are used when the interviewee responds.

6. Why is this challenge/why are these challenges important for you to solve?

Observe key words, emphasis and behaviours that are used when the interviewee responds.

7. What is your current solution, and how did you discover this solution?

Observe key words, emphasis and behaviours that are used when the interviewee responds.

8. What would you like to improve/what do you think needs to be improved about your current solution?

Observe key words, emphasis and behaviours that are used when the interviewee responds.

9. We are currently working a solution to this problem; will you be interested in giving feedback/testing?

Observe key words, emphasis and behaviours that are used when the interviewee responds.

Copyright material from Hirani & Varin 2003, *Supporting Adult Learners through Games and Interactive Teaching*, Routledge

10. Are there other persons you know who need this problem to be solved or who depend on the solution?

Observe key words, emphasis and behaviours that are used when the interviewee responds.

Thank them for their time and contribution. This exercise will give you a deeper insight into the opportunity you are trying to capture and the problem you are trying to solve.

15.3 Adaptation of the Games to a Different Context

The customer discovery process can be applied to different types of business models and to for-profit as well as non-profit organisation forms.

- **For-profit ventures**

  Customer discovery can take place in Business-to-Business (B2B) as well as Business-to-Consumer (B2C) business situations for for-profit organisations that are looking to solve a problem in the market or to capitalise on an identified opportunity.

- **Non-profit solutions**

  In the case where interventions are being delivered by non-profits or where solutions are sought for community issues, the customer discovery approach can help to better understand and align interventions towards the needs of beneficiaries and stakeholders in the communities where the intervening organisation is seeking to do work.

Bibliography

Blank, S. (2013). *The four steps to the epiphany*. 1st ed. Menlo Park: K & S Ranch Publishing LLC.

Cooper, S. B. (2004). Stepping out of the classroom and up the ladder of learning: An experiential learning approach to entrepreneurship education. *Industry and Higher Education*, 18(1), pp. 11–22.

Fenwick, Tara J. (2001). *Experiential learning: a theoretical critique from five perspectives*. Information Series No. 385. Columbus, OH: Center on Education and Training for Employment.

Kolb, D. (1984) *Experiential learning: experience as the source of learning and development*. Englewood Cliffs, New Jersey: Prentice Hall.

Copyright material from Hirani & Varin 2003, *Supporting Adult Learners through Games and Interactive Teaching*, Routledge

16 Teaching Students How to Network
Goal-setting, Maintenance and Technology

Sven Botha

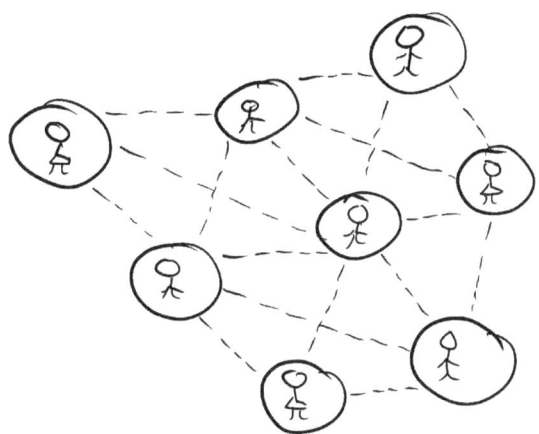

16.1 Overview

Networking is considered essential for professional development and the overall success of one's career, with 88% of professionals holding this point of view (Kimberl 2020). Similarly, this view is held by a number of scholars who study the impact of networking and its causal link to success later in life. See, for example, Brown (1999), Spurk et al. (2015) and Kuwabara et al. (2020). Yet, students tend to struggle with the very idea and activity of networking. As Hinkley (n.d.) reflects, "Being a busy and slightly shy student, I found networking to be challenging, even when given specific recommendations for people with whom to connect". The intersection of both of these realities calls for the development of an approach to teaching which emphasises the importance of networking while also enabling students to overcome their fears. This chapter introduces students to the concept of networking as a goal-orientated process that requires planning, maintenance and, at times, quick thinking. Viewing networking as a process, instead of a single activity, will teach students how to sustain a connection once it has been established, how to identify the additional benefits of networking in addition to growing their list of contacts and how to find value in connections from outside of their own field of study. The activity proposed in this chapter, something the author terms the Networking Goal, employs a goal-orientated approach to growing a professional network. A goal-orientated approach refers to being able to reflect on one's past actions with the aim of learning from failures and successes to improve one's skill set, mastery of new situations and overall competency levels (Wang et al. 2021).

To properly understand how the networking process links to goal-orientated learning, one first has to have a working definition of networking. While networking is the process by which someone forms connections, the way these connections get formed differ from context to context. On a personal level, networking is a means of establishing connections that one can ask reciprocal favours from (Indeed 2021). A more formal and business-like definition of networking refers to "sets of connected exchange relationships between actors (individuals, firms, universities, government agencies, and other organisations) to create and share knowledge, capabilities and resources in order to accelerate the process of successful innovation and commercialisation and to create competitive advantage" (Maghsoudi-Ganjeh et al. 2021, 53 and 54). While both of these definitions provide insight into what networking is, they fall short of viewing networking as a process. In response, this chapter defines networking as a process whereby an individual seeks to establish a series of connections with multiple actors which require maintenance to yield maximum mutual benefit.

The activity this chapter proposes is based on some professional experiences the author has had while negotiating his academic career path as a fledgling academic. The Networking Goal is an activity that can be facilitated within groups of various sizes.[1] Moreover, the Networking Goal can be applied to various professional settings, such as, but not limited to, academia, diplomacy and business. The incorporation of technologies such as LinkedIn and Twitter will also be demonstrated.

16.2 Game Details

16.2.1 Key Skills

Establishing connections, retaining connections, planning, critical thinking, creative thinking, communication

16.2.2 Group Size

For smaller groups: 4–16 students
For larger groups: 20 plus
Even numbers work best

16.2.3 Time

For smaller groups: three to four weeks (this activity could be a practical assignment for small groups of postgraduate students)

For larger groups: 30–60 minutes depending on the duration of your lecture/tutorial and the size of your group

16.2.4 Purpose (Learning Objectives)

1. To help students develop a systematic means of networking
2. To encourage students to plan for their interactions to yield the most out of their networking efforts
3. To teach students how to identify mutual benefit or value with people outside of their own area(s) of knowledge
4. To encourage students to see the potential for creative solutions, via their network, to societal problems
5. To encourage students to use various social media platforms to advance their networking abilities

16.2.5 Preparation and Setup

For smaller groups:

- Print copies of Material 1 that are equivalent to the number of students you have in class.
- In an online space, Material 1 can be distributed by online learning platforms such as Moodle or Blackboard in MS Word format or as a PDF document.
- Make sure that your students are familiar with LinkedIn.

For larger groups:

- Make sure each group has sufficient space to deliberate.
- Depending on the size of the class, the instructor may wish to brief and/or practice the Networking Goal with your tutors/teaching assistants beforehand so that they can help administer the activity during class.

16.2.6 Instructions

16.2.6.1 Instructions for Larger Groups

Students will be engaging in a role-play activity to learn how to grow their professional networks. The Networking Goal assumes that all role players have a value-adding role to play in achieving a goal. The following scenario outlines the roles assigned to role players.

Activity Brief: The scenario in this **activity** is an engagement between **the primary networker (the person seeking to grow their network)** and **two to three secondary networkers (usually people who are well placed within their own originations to assist the primary networker in achieving their goal)**. The nature of the roles each of the participants takes on and the circumstances under which they interact will be determined by the scenario chosen by the instructor (see Section 16.3). The principal objective for the primary networker is to try and get the secondary networkers to join their network.

Students should not share details of their roles and scenarios with anyone else. Students will be given a fixed amount of time to role-play and act out their roles. At the end of this time, students will reconvene in a plenary to have a debrief and share the outcomes of their group and individual interactions.

Read the activity brief to the students.

Divide students into groups of three or four and assign them the role of the primary and secondary networker. There should only be one participant assigned to the former role.

Important: participants should not see or learn of each other's roles beforehand.

Once all of the roles have been assigned, students should be given 3–5 minutes to study the role they have been assigned.

Following this time allocation, students should be given 20 minutes to interact with each other. The goal of this interaction should be for all of the participants to introduce themselves and their roles; the primary networker should try to determine how the secondary networkers can feed into their network.

Not all of the information pertaining to the participants should be revealed within the first line of dialogue. Instead, the primary and secondary networkers should engage in an open exchange that builds insight, trust and understanding.

Students need to uphold certain rules of engagement, which are dictated by the scenario they have been given by the instructor.

Following the 20-minute duration, participants should be given between 3 and 5 minutes to note down some brief reflections. These reflections should be twofold.

Firstly, the individual participants should reflect on their own performance. Here the guiding questions should be:

- → What did you learn from this experience?
- → What were my strengths during this interaction?
- → What were my weaknesses during this exchange?

Secondly, the group should reflect on their own performance. Here the guiding questions should be:

- → Were we able to establish a common ground that allowed us to work together?
- → What were the reasons for common ground occurring or not occurring?
- → Did common ground occur, but with limitations?

(Instructors should note that the outcomes implied in the preceding questions may occur throughout an interaction).

Each group of participants must elect a 'spokesperson' to deliver feedback on the group's behalf during the debrief session.

Participants may share their individual reflections if they wish to do so and if time permits; however, these are mostly used for personal reflection, which can be useful should the Networking Goal be carried out two or three times in the semester.

16.2.6.2 Instructions for Smaller Groups

Smaller groups present the instructor with the opportunity to employ a remote approach to networking in which students are taught how to leverage social media for networking purposes. Key to this activity is how students can enhance their networking capabilities in a relatively cost-effective way.[2] Networking via social media platforms, particularly LinkedIn, yields more promising professional results (Utz and Breuer 2019).

Activity Brief: The scenario in this **activity** is an engagement between **the primary networker (the student learning how to use LinkedIn)** and at least one **secondary networker (usually people who are well placed within their own originations to assist the primary networker in achieving their goal)**. The primary goal of this activity will be for the student to engage a possible new connection via LinkedIn for over a period of time to establish a rapport and yield opportunities for themselves.

Students should use Material 1 to record their progress. The student's ability to reflect and learn from their online experience should help them achieve their goal of becoming a better networker. Any student new to the LinkedIn platform or seeking further guidance on the platform works should approach their instructor.

Read the activity brief outlined above to the students.

Give students three to five days to identify a connection they would like to make. It is important that the identified connection aligns with the student's career objectives and trajectory. The lengthy allocation of time for this phase of the activity is necessary, particularly for those students who need to put aside time to think about their career objectives.

Administer a short overview of what LinkedIn is and how it should be used.

Once the students have identified their preferred connection, they should be given a set timeframe (two to three weeks) within which to establish meaningful contact with their connection.

Each student should be provided with a copy of Material 1 to record their progress on. The idea behind this table is for students to regard their desired goal and their progress towards that goal by working backwards towards establishing a meaningful contract with their new connection.

During this time period, it is important that the student explore the various features of LinkedIn (i.e., LinkedIn Messenger, the various sections and sub-sections of the LinkedIn profile and the short courses offered by LinkedIn and other platforms).

Students should be prepared to identify two or three possible connections in case the primary connection is unresponsive.

It is important to place emphasis on the fact that students will not solely be assessed on the outcome of their engagements on LinkedIn and that reflective and adaptive attitudes also count towards the end result.

Students should be advised that they will need to provide elements of proof as part of their assessment to verify that the interactions did take place. This can be done in person via brief consultation with the instructor towards the end of the assessment period. Screenshots should be a last resort so as to safeguard the secondary networker's privacy.

16.2.6.3 Guidance (Smaller Groups Only*)

Students may be tempted to look at the background of each of the role players before they engage. This is not allowed to happen as getting to know 'new' people is part of the networking process.

Make sure that the group sizes are relatively small. Large groups tend to extend the exchange, which can place time allocations under strain.

Students may not wish to share their self-identified weaknesses/challenges. Remind students that learning from weaknesses and challenges is part of the learning process.

*Be mindful that some of your students may approach you for guidance on how to set up a LinkedIn profile or guidance on how to use LinkedIn effectively. Be prepared to provide guidance or ask a tutor or teaching assistant to assist.

*Some students may wish to undertake the Networking Goal by engaging with their classmates instead of a new connection. This should be prevented. The objective is to meet new people for professional purposes.

16.2.6.4 Debrief (Smaller Groups Only*)

Once the main activity concludes, instructors should gather students, in an in-person or online meeting, to share their experiences. Some guiding questions for the debrief may include:

Who were the secondary networkers in your scenario?

What were the rules of engagement in your scenario; did these rules make it harder for you to establish a connection with your contact?

What would you say are the unforeseen or hidden benefits of networking for you as a student?

If you were given the opportunity to redo the exercise, what about yourself as the networker would you change?

If you were able to establish a new connection via a secondary networker, what arrangements did you make to maintain it?

*Do you feel that you have a better understanding of how technology can aid you in your networking endeavours?

*What, in your view, are the benefits and drawbacks of using technology to network?

16.2.7 Handouts and Material

16.2.7.1 Material 1: Keeping Track of Your Networking Progress

Tracking Your Progress at Networking

Activity	Timeframe	Student's reflections
(Actions needed to achieve your goal, including sub-goals, should be noted down here)	(Due dates should be noted here; students should work backwards towards achieving their goals)	(Students should include their strengths, weaknesses, and challenges)

16.3 Adaptation to a Different Context

Networking is an essential skill that can be employed across various settings. This section houses different scenarios that can be used by the instructor depending on the courses they teach. Each scenario has specific rules of engagement that must be adhered to. Actions ensure that the diversity of networking is well understood. Brief notes are also provided discussing how the Networking Goal can also be applied to the specific field via the academic lens.

- *Scenario 1: The Ambassador's residence*

The primary networker is a musician at the Cuban Ambassador's Residence by invitation to commutate Cuban Independence Day. The musician is concerned with how the mainstream media portrays Cuba and decides to try and

Copyright material from Hirani & Varin 2003, *Supporting Adult Learners through Games and Interactive Teaching*, Routledge

rectify the situation by helping Cuba amplify its use of cultural diplomacy via musical means. Also in attendance is the CEO of a major record label and a well-known marketing agent. Attempt to address your concern by eliciting the assistance of other guests in attendance.

- *Scenario 2: The humanitarian crisis*

An earthquake has just struck the small island state in which you are a local schoolteacher. Many of your students, their friends and their families are gravely injured. The healthcare and emergency response teams of the small island state are overstretched. In your panic, you try to leverage the help of a volunteer with Doctors Without Borders and a junior United Nations volunteer. There is a strong possibility that an aftershock will strike within the next 15 minutes. You, as the primary networker, must try to attempt to save those most injured and help to bring more aid to the scene from the international community.

- *Scenario 3: The new deal*

You, as the primary networker, are a new intern at a national marketing firm. You have four months left on your internship and are worried about what you will do once your internship comes to an end. Your firm holds a client mixer, which you are invited to attend. While at the mixer, you are approached by an entrepreneur who may have a new invention. Deep in conversation, two more of your fellow interns join the two of you. Attempt to secure a new opportunity from the entrepreneur without isolating your fellow interns.

Notes

1 The author's reflections, which helped to formulate the Networking Goal, were drawn from a joint experience of tutoring and lecturing in a setting with large undergraduate groups and small postgraduate groups.
2 The author is aware that high data costs in some parts of the Global South make it challenging for students to access online platforms. Regardless, it stands to reason that certain social media platforms such as LinkedIn remain a priority as students search for opportunities.

Bibliography

Brown, J. (1999). The professional and personal value of networking. *Australian Journal of Learning Difficulties*, 4(3), pp. 35–8.

Hinkley, L. (n.d.). The networking challenge. Career Centre, School of Education, University of Wisconsin-Madison. Available from: https://careercenter.education.wisc.edu/students-alumni/prepare-and-connect/networking/the-networking-challenge/. Accessed: 7 January 2022.

Indeed. (2021). Professional networking: what it is and how to master it. Available from: https://www.indeed.com/career-advice/career-development/professional-networking. Accessed: 14 November 2021.

Kimberl, M. (2020). Infographic: the challenge of remote networking for college students. *Multi Briefs*. Available from: http://exclusive.multibriefs.com/content/infographic-the-challenge-of-remote-networking-for-college-students/education. Accessed: 12 November 2021.

Kuwabara, K., Zou, X., Aven, B., Hildebrand, C. and Iyengar, S. (2020). Lay theories of networking ability: beliefs that inhibit instrumental networking. *Social Networks*, 62, pp. 1–11.

Maghsoudi-Ganjeh, Y., Khani, N. and Alem-Tabriz, A. (2021). Networking capability commercialisation performance: *The role of network structure*. *Journal of Business-to-Business Marketing*, 28(1): 51–68.

Spurk, D., Kauffeld, S., Barthauer, L. and Heinemann, N.S.R. (2015). Fostering networking behavior, career planning and optimism, and subjective career success: an intervention study. *Journal of Vocational Behaviour*, 87, pp. 134–44.

Utz, S. and Breuer, J. (2019). The relationship between networking, LinkedIn use, and retrieving informational benefits. *Cyberpsychology, Behavior, and Social Networking*, 22(3), pp. 180–5.

Wang, W., Song, S. and Yuan, W. (2021). When learning goal orientation leads to learning from failure: the roles of negative emotion coping orientation and positive grieving. *Frontiers in Psychology*, Advanced online publication.

17 Conclusion

17.1 Why This Book and Why Now

This book is the culmination of many years spent teaching through play. It is the result of hours of discussions between the authors to devise a user-friendly way to package this for educators who are embracing this effective teaching style. These chapters have covered a myriad of ways that play can be used to deliver learning outcomes in adult education. The book's contributors have come from across the world, including Asia, Africa, Europe and North America, making this a holistic and global contribution to the field of learning through play.

The spark that led to the realisation of this book was one of the authors having spent time teaching in an alternative education school in London that caters to students with severe behavioural issues who have been excluded from mainstream education in the UK. Engaging these teenagers through games in order to learn soft skills such as communication and teamwork proved to be an effective approach in helping the students achieve better behavioural outcomes. This experience played a part in the authors' joint decision to write this book in the form of a toolkit filled with fun and educative games. As discussed in the introduction, games and play are effective learning tools for children and adults alike but have not been explored in depth amongst adults, especially in higher education. This book intends to offer interested educators a toolkit of easy-to-use games that can be modified to suit different contexts. The book also reduces the barriers of entry for educators interested in engaging in play for learning for adults but may not have much experience with it. The authors hope this book will spark a revolution in how we achieve learning outcomes in adult education.

The COVID-19 pandemic has affected the education sector significantly with learning having moved online across the world, forcing educators to find creative ways to keep students engaged virtually. This book has been written at a time when many educators worldwide were forced to revisit their teaching styles. Many found ways to incorporate virtual games into their teaching, shifting their perspectives on how we educate. As we begin to come out of the

DOI: 10.4324/9781003230120-17

pandemic, the way we engage with work and education has been permanently altered, and creative ways to teach students will need to enter the classrooms once students return to in-person learning. This book is well positioned to provide these educators with a way to engage with the concept of Play to Learn without needing to design from scratch.

17.2 What We Mean by "Play"

A variety of types of play have been used in this book ranging from the classic use of board games and card games such as Monopoly to experiential-based play, which includes role-playing and immersive activities mirroring real-life scenarios. Play has been described in the introduction as "a sequence of events where the player is at times in control and at times out of control, creating a cognitively complex emotional state that we call 'having fun'". All the chapters in the book outline games that are covered by this definition and in addition to the participants having fun while playing, they are learning and developing specific skills. This is the value brought by this book. The introduction also highlights that play is both instinctive and natural for mammals, which further supports the idea that learning through play should come naturally to us at all ages, not just as children.

17.3 What Next

This book has been the first step to developing the Play to Learn space for adults. Through writing the book, the authors are cognisant of the fact that it will encourage unfamiliar educators to experiment with the games in the chapters. This experimentation is made easier by the simplicity of most of the games and the short amount of time needed to understand each game before using it in a classroom. It will also provide more familiar educators with a set of ready-designed games to pick up without having to spend significant amounts of time on the design process. The next step will be to ensure that these educators are appropriately trained to deliver education through interactive methods, particularly through play. While exposing educators is important and valuable, it is imperative that they are implementing these tools effectively. Therefore, training the trainers is a natural next step to evolve this growing community of Play to Learn educators.

17.4 Play to Learn Educators Unite

It is clear that the education landscape is changing. The Future of Work demands skilled workers, and higher education needs to shift focus to skills development in order to meet these demands. Technology has also transformed the means of transferring knowledge and reinvented the role of teachers in a classroom. Engaging and motivating students in a sustained manner are critical to the educator's relevance in the Digital Age. While the jobs of the future are unknown, the ability to learn throughout one's life now defines the essence of education. What better way to keep learning than by enjoying the process? Learning through play is one effective method to achieve this, and educators around the world should embrace this easy and low-cost mode of education.

Index

action research 9, 97–100, 103–4
active 3, 25–6, 39, 48, 50, 96–7, 106, 113, 142, 153–5, 159, 173
active listening 9, 48, 142, 153, 155
activities 6, 39–40, 47, 50, 54, 89, 95–7, 104, 117, 125, 154–5, 173
activity 2, 25–7, 35, 40, 42, 47–8, 50–1, 53–4, 84, 96–7, 99, 103, 104, 108, 115–8, 121–5, 145, 150, 154, 156, 158, 163–9
adult 1–3, 5, 10, 84, 135, 155, 172–3
algorithm 58, 65, 76–8
analogy 14, 19
analysis 8, 22, 25, 38, 59, 71, 100, 103, 155
analytical 3, 16, 58–9
applied 6, 15, 50, 58, 98, 103–4, 117, 124–5, 133, 141, 155, 162, 164, 169

bankrupt 72, 75
bankrupting 73, 75
brain 2, 136, 138–140, 147
brainstorm 99–101, 149, 151
business 5–8, 20, 30–1, 46–7, 49–50, 53–4, 127, 141, 154, 156, 162, 164

challenges 3, 5–6, 23, 33, 49–50, 81, 161, 168–9
Chance 60–1, 64, 66–73, 76
cognitive 2, 4–6, 10, 33, 82–3, 94–5, 116, 173
collaborate 147, 151
collaborative 5, 31, 47, 96, 148
communication 3, 5, 7, 9, 13, 20, 26, 41, 83, 97, 101, 107, 108, 112, 117–8, 124, 136, 141–9, 153, 164, 172
Community Chest 60–1, 64, 66–73, 76
competition 42, 47–8, 50, 107, 123
complex 1–2, 4–5, 8, 22, 25–6, 33, 38–9
complexity 8–10, 31, 54

complimentary 8–9
conceptualise 32
conflict 4, 13, 15, 21, 46, 137, 140
connection 14, 35, 115, 163–4, 167–8
Constructivism 16, 20, 22, 40, 84
context 1, 5–10, 14, 20, 22, 29–30, 40, 45, 49, 54, 58, 82–3, 93, 103, 114, 116–7, 122–5, 133, 143, 153, 159, 162, 164, 169, 172
cooperate 14–5, 17–22
cooperation 8, 14, 16, 20–1, 44, 49, 73, 106–7, 141
creative 3, 7, 30, 43, 85, 103, 141, 147, 153, 164–5, 172–3
crisis 7–8, 22, 38, 40, 42, 44–5, 170
critical 3, 5, 7–8, 15, 39, 50, 53, 59, 71, 81–4, 94–5, 103, 144, 152, 164, 174
critical inquiry 8, 82–3, 95
culture 1, 14, 38, 49, 107
customer 9, 31, 48–50, 52–4, 56, 154–160, 162

data 8, 58–9, 82, 97–100, 103, 144, 148, 170
debrief 17, 19, 21, 26–8, 33, 35–6, 43–4, 51, 53, 66, 89, 98, 107, 111, 112–3, 116–7, 121, 123, 130, 132, 137, 144–5, 146–7, 149–151, 153, 156, 158–9, 166–8
decision-making 7–8, 14–6, 21–2, 58, 60, 65–6, 80, 117, 136, 138, 148–9
deconstruction 83
define 53, 59, 79, 142, 144–5, 157–8, 164, 174
defined 5, 25, 48, 73–4
design thinking 9, 141–2, 145, 152–3
dialogue 3, 14, 47, 83–4, 107, 166
dice 59, 62–3, 64, 66, 69–76, 79
didactic 3, 6
digital 4–5, 174

discipline 1, 7, 9, 14, 22, 116
discussion 3, 17, 19, 21, 33, 36, 41, 43, 49, 59, 63, 75, 88–9, 100, 103, 112–3, 115, 123, 131, 152, 172
distribution 7, 63–4, 75–7, 79
distributive 25–9, 31

economics 7–8, 17, 25, 32, 33
economy 33–6
education 1–7, 13, 26, 47, 82, 84, 95, 97, 141, 155, 172–4
educator 1, 4–10, 14–7, 19, 26, 33–4, 36, 40–2, 42–5, 50, 94, 96–8, 117, 127, 130, 172–4
emotions 13, 15–7, 21, 135–6, 138
emotional intelligence 135–6, 142
empathise 21, 53, 142–4, 150
empathy 4, 9, 47–50, 52, 141–4
employee 4, 6, 26, 84
employer 25–6
entrepreneur 50, 53, 155–8, 170
entrepreneurial 47–8, 51, 53, 155
entrepreneurship 9, 49–50, 154–5, 159
experience 1–5, 7, 15, 22, 26, 28, 32–3, 39, 44, 47, 49, 53, 82, 97, 98–100, 113, 116–7, 124, 126, 141, 143, 151, 154

facilitator 44, 48–9, 51, 53–4, 60–1, 107, 109, 111–8, 121, 123, 137, 141, 153, 158–9
feedback 5, 16, 40, 44, 49, 56, 82–3, 94, 98, 103, 135, 138, 147–8, 152–3, 156–161, 167
Feminism 21, 23, 40
finance 26, 49
flexibility 9, 19, 141, 144
FOMO 97–8, 101, 104
frequency 63–4, 72, 76–7
fun 2, 32–3, 48, 54, 83, 94, 106, 108, 111, 116, 118, 136, 138, 151, 172–3

games-based 1, 6–7, 13, 38
gamification 33, 141
governance 7, 127–8
grid 106–112, 114–8, 121–3, 125

handouts 7, 27–9, 44, 89, 100, 125, 132, 135, 140, 159, 169
history 3, 8, 19–20, 22, 81–3, 93, 95
hotspot 116–7

imagination 54, 107
improvement 5, 44, 50, 100, 156

incentive 7, 15, 20, 33, 127
income 34–6, 61, 66, 68–70, 72, 78
inflation 8, 33–5, 58, 80
information 3, 5, 15, 19, 29–30, 40, 81–3, 85, 94–7, 99, 103–4, 110, 117, 126–8, 132–3, 137–140, 143, 148, 152, 166
information asymmetry 126–7, 132
instructions 3, 7, 9, 15, 17, 27, 34, 42, 51–2, 60, 66, 76, 86, 99, 107, 109, 121–2, 127–9, 135–7, 143–5, 147, 149–152, 156, 165, 167
integrative 5, 26–9, 31
interactive 7, 9, 13, 48
international 7–8, 13, 15–6, 20–3, 31, 38, 40–6, 81, 170
international relations 7–8, 13, 22–3, 31, 38, 40, 81
interview 27, 99–100, 102, 104, 155–162
intuitive 13–4, 16–7, 147
IR theories 13–7, 19–22, 38–43
iterate 51, 56
iteration 50, 56, 155

knowledge 2–7, 13, 15, 17, 22–3, 26, 32, 38–9, 41, 48, 60, 83, 94–5, 98, 115–6, 154–5, 164–5, 173

leadership 5, 7, 26, 36, 54, 99, 117–8, 125, 135
learn
learner-centred
learning 1–7, 13, 15–7, 19–21, 25–6, 29, 32–4, 38–41, 44, 47–51, 53–4, 59, 81–4, 86, 94–8, 104, 106, 108, 113, 116–8, 121, 123, 126, 128, 135–6, 140–1, 143–8, 150–6, 164–5, 167–8, 172–4
lecture 3, 4, 7, 15, 16, 21, 39, 135, 137–8, 159
Liberalism 16, 20, 22
logic 7, 14, 16, 20, 85

Mafia 20, 126, 133
manual 7, 10
market 7, 34–6, 49–50, 52–3, 60, 154–5, 162
material 6–7, 23, 27–30, 42, 44, 50–1, 54, 83, 86, 89, 92, 100–2, 106–9, 112–3, 118, 122, 125, 132, 135, 140, 144–7, 149–153, 156, 159, 165, 167
method 3–4, 6–7, 47, 49–50, 58, 60–4, 71–3, 76–7, 79, 83–4, 95, 122, 124, 148, 154–5, 173–4
metrics 59–60, 66, 73

military 22, 42–5
mocktail 47–8, 52, 55–6
money 8, 33–6, 73, 75, 80
Monopoly 8, 34, 58, 60, 62, 80, 173
motivate 1, 21, 50–1
motivational 2, 5–6, 33, 82

Narrator 127–132
negotiate 25, 27–9, 54
negotiation 8, 15, 25–31, 49, 131
network 1, 49, 166
networking 9, 163–5, 167–171
neurological 2, 10
non-verbal 117–8, 122–4

objective 16, 22, 26–8, 34, 41–3, 45–6, 50, 59, 61, 72–3, 75, 84, 98, 103, 108, 118, 121, 123, 128, 136, 143–8, 150–2, 156, 165–8

pandemics 38–9, 41–4
pedagogical 4, 6–7, 14, 51, 96–7
pedagogy 7, 82, 94–5
peer 5, 15, 19, 32, 47, 49, 50, 97–8, 103, 109, 135, 137
performance 5, 51, 59–60, 66, 155, 166
persona 25, 143, 150
perspective 8, 15, 26, 44, 47–8, 82–6, 88, 92–5, 118, 136
physical 2, 10, 102, 104, 109, 143
play 1, 3, 8–10, 16–7, 23, 25–7, 29–30, 33, 44, 52, 58, 66, 82, 85, 96–8, 104
player 2, 17, 50, 58–66, 69, 71–80, 84–9, 107–8, 110–2, 114–5, 126–133, 151, 153, 165, 168, 173
playful 17, 42, 47–8, 50, 54, 107
plenary 19, 21, 27–8, 33, 43, 66, 136–7, 166
policy 32–4, 127
politics 14, 21, 32, 40, 82
power 5, 8, 22–3, 44, 64, 82–3, 126–8, 131
practical 1, 3, 7, 26, 58, 100, 150, 154, 158, 165
prisoner's dilemma 8, 13, 14–5, 17, 22
problem-based 38, 96
problem-solving 5, 7–8, 14, 40, 106–7, 117–8, 121, 124, 141, 145–7, 153, 155
product 2, 9, 30, 33, 48–9, 50, 86–7, 93, 155–9
property 58–60, 62, 64–7, 69, 73, 75, 77–80
prototype 142, 151–2, 157
prototyping 149, 151–2, 155
psychology 50, 126, 132, 138

rapport 127
rational 15, 22, 138–9
rationale 19, 94
rationality 13, 16
real-world 5, 8, 15–6, 35, 40, 43, 47–8, 154
Realism 16, 19–20, 22, 40–5
reasoning 14, 85, 86, 88, 92, 117–8, 138
reflection 15, 25, 52, 85, 95, 107, 114, 116, 155, 166–7, 169–170
reflective 84, 95, 98, 117, 124, 152, 154, 156, 168
research 2, 4–6, 9, 52–3, 83, 96–100, 103–4
risk-free 5, 39
role play 25–6

scenario 8, 14–7, 19–22, 25–31, 34, 39–40, 42–5, 75, 89, 152, 154, 156–160, 165–170, 173
Sceptic 86, 88, 92–3
self-reflection 5, 113
simulating 5, 154
simulation 5, 25–7, 38–40, 42–5, 76
skills 1–10, 13–4, 16, 25–6, 29, 33, 38–40, 44, 48–50, 54, 58–9, 82–4, 89, 97–8, 103, 107–8, 112–3, 116–8, 125, 127, 136, 141–150, 152–6, 164, 169, 172–3
social 5–6, 8–9, 13, 19–22, 32, 35, 42, 45, 48, 56, 81–2, 84–5, 94–101, 104, 126, 135, 138, 153, 165, 167, 170
social media 9, 48, 56, 96–101, 104, 165, 167
social science 8, 81–2, 84, 94, 135, 138
sociocultural 33
solution 48, 50, 122, 141, 144–5, 148, 150–2, 154–162, 165
start-up 9, 47, 49–50, 53, 154
statistical 58
strategy 7–8, 19, 28–31, 58–9, 97–8, 108, 124, 145
student 1, 3–7, 9–10, 13–7, 19–22, 25–8, 31–6, 39–45, 51, 54–5, 58–64, 71, 73–4, 76, 78–9, 83–5, 95–6–100, 102–4, 106–9, 113, 116–7, 123, 126–8, 135, 138, 140–1, 153–9, 163–170, 172–3
system 3–4, 20–1, 23, 49, 86, 88, 92–3, 107–8, 138–9

teaching 1–7, 9, 13, 17, 26, 38–9, 48, 83–4, 94, 97, 113, 163, 168, 172
team-building 54, 84, 106

teamwork 7, 113, 117, 125, 141, 145, 148, 150, 172
technology 5, 41, 58, 94, 98, 118, 163, 168, 173
tenet 8, 13–6, 19, 21–2, 42, 44
test 28, 53, 56, 142, 152, 157, 159
testing 52–3, 56, 141, 152, 155–7, 159, 161
theories 8, 13–7, 19–22, 38, 22, 38–44
thinking 2–5, 7–9, 23, 39, 50, 59, 62, 66, 84–5, 88, 94–5, 103, 138–9, 141–6, 148–9, 151–3, 163–4
Toffeconomy 32, 34
toffee 33–6
tool 2, 5, 10, 14, 26, 33, 38–9, 48, 81, 95–8, 126, 149, 153, 172–3
toolkit 7, 172
trading 33, 60–1, 64–6, 73

training 1–2, 5–7, 141, 173
transfer 8, 29, 82
transferable 1, 14, 16, 38–40, 83
trust 19–21, 126–8, 132, 135–6, 148, 166
trust-building 9

verbal 104, 118
Villager 127–8, 130–2
virtual 51, 85, 94, 172
visualisation 43, 58–9, 63, 143

wealth 21, 35–6, 60–2, 72–5
Werewolf 126–7, 130–3
win-win 27, 29, 31
worksheet 99–102, 156–7, 159–160

zombie 39–43

For Product Safety Concerns and Information please contact our EU representative GPSR@taylorandfrancis.com
Taylor & Francis Verlag GmbH, Kaufingerstraße 24, 80331 München, Germany

www.ingramcontent.com/pod-product-compliance
Lightning Source LLC
Chambersburg PA
CBHW071204240426
43668CB00032B/2096